What He Says Where He Sends

'Messages given at Keswick have brought spiritual enlightenment, refreshment and challenge to God's people all over the world. So I welcome the launch of The New Keswick Collection.'
John Stott

'God meets with many people and they with Him at Keswick year by year. I am delighted that the great themes of the Convention are now being more fully put down into print that many others may also meet with God and He with them.'
Michael A. Baughen
Bishop of Chester

'I warmly commend this new series.'
Eric J. Alexander

☐ New Keswick Collection ☐

Forthcoming titles in this series:
The Holy Spirit, David Jackman
Becoming Like Christ, Charles Price
Discipleship, Raymond Brown

What He Says, Where He Sends

A New Challenge to Mission and Service

Philip Hacking

Marshall Pickering

Marshall Morgan and Scott
Marshall Pickering
3 Beggarwood Lane, Basingstoke,
Hants RG23 7LP, UK

First published in 1988 by Marshall Morgan and Scott
Publications Ltd
Part of the Marshall Pickering Holdings Group
A subsidiary of the Zondervan Corporation

ISBN 0 551 01634 5

Text set in Plantin by Watermark,
Hampermill Cottage, Watford WD1 4PL
Printed in Great Britain by Richard Clay, Bungay,
Suffolk

Contents

Endorsement

It is always a joy to endorse a bible centred volume and this is certainly that. I am equally delighted to commend a volume on Mission since the church is "the only society on earth that exists primarily for its non-members". The question we need to be asking is not "Why should I go?", but "Why should I stay where I am?". The Christian attitude whatever the age or status must always be determined by the question "Am I in the place God has put me, fulfilling the task God has given me?". Philip Hacking's book will help to focus mind and heart on these issues.

Rev. Jim Graham

Preface

For well over 100 years the Keswick Convention has been expounding the truth of scripture in that lovely Lakeland setting. It may be, humanly speaking, an act of coincidence that the Vicar of Keswick discovered the reality of new life in the Spirit. Generations since have been thrilled that this discovery was made by someone who could begin a movement in that part of Britain where it is so easy to be aware of the presence of a great and majestic God.

The Keswick Convention has emphasised over these years the centrality of the life of holiness in the believer. With great confidence in the authority of scripture, successive generations of men from all denominations have been used by the Spirit of God in expounding the Word of God to lead people closer to the Lord himself and to experience the reality of the fullness of the Spirit. From time to time books have been written by Keswick speakers expanding that message. It is the aim of this new series to take some of the great themes of Keswick, make them relevant to our contemporary world and to show how they fit into the total ministry of the church of Jesus Christ. In this way it is hoped that the ministry of the Convention will be multiplied. We trust that it may lead more people to want to share in the unique ministry at the Convention itself but even more to understand, enjoy and respond to the central messages of the Convention.

The message of the Keswick Convention has spread throughout the world and it is perhaps significant that this opening book in the series takes up the theme of Mission and Service. It is no coincidence that a Convention which majors on holiness will inevitably lead to a call to service. Christian holiness is no cloistered virtue but a call to live in the world as men and women who are separated from the world and yet have a world-transforming message and mission. It is nothing less than the call to follow our Lord not only in his teaching but in his way of life.

So we launch this series in the hope that year by year titles will appear enabling people of all ages to enjoy these truths which have transformed the lives of so many of us and which it is a privilege to expound not only at Keswick, but in the local church and in every part of the world where the message of Keswick has gone with great power and conviction.

Philip H. Hacking

Acknowledgement

The author wishes to acknowledge warmly the help given in research for the details in Chapter 7 by Ian Enticott, now himself on missionary service in Tanzania. It is appropriate that the work of investigating some of the history of the Keswick Convention in the missionary enterprise should be done by one who himself had heard that call of God to work overseas.

1: Comings and Goings

Memories can play tricks. But my abiding recollection of the the only Keswick Convention I ever attended on the audience side is not of stirring Bible Readings, nor of great messages, although no doubt these were there in abundance. I remember most vividly the uncomfortable challenge of the missionary meeting and my fiancée and myself believing it would be right to stand as a commitment to the Lord for full-time service wherever and whenever He might call.

It is an amazing twist of the the Lord's providence that I am now called as Chairman of the Council to make that appeal, and it is still the most moving part of any Convention.

In my hazy recollection the call to service was linked with an exposition of Isaiah chapter 6. Once more the Lord does strange things. I can remember well enough the particular challenge of that chapter without recollecting when or by whom it was preached. But I learned then, and I have often relearned it and conveyed it to others, that God actually invited the prophet to serve. There was no forcing, no compulsion. The Lord asked, 'Whom shall I send and who will go for us?' I realised then that I was given the privilege of saying yes or no to the Lord, and the Lord gave me the grace to say with Isaiah,

1

'Here am I, send me.'

My situation was very unlike Isaiah's at that moment. The only comparable factor was that I too was a young man eager to serve. But as yet I had no great prophetic calling. Eighteen months would pass before I heard the call in a church in Oxford to the ordained ministry in the Church of England, and I knew instinctively that this was the Lord's answer to my commitment in the tent at Keswick.

If I had been asked how all this linked with the Keswick message on the theme of holiness of life and the lordship of Jesus, I would have been unsure how to answer. Nor could I have fitted it all into the week's scheme of teaching and the preparation for the Communion Service in the evening. Nor was I privileged in those days to have the effective follow-up of a Christian Service Centre. Some things may not have improved over the years but some have improved enormously. We do care now to follow up all these commitments and I believe that we are absolutely right. Nonetheless when God has his hand upon a person even the absence of careful follow-up can be overruled. When God deals with you, there can be few doubts.

It would be impossible to estimate the thousands of people who have gone out from Keswick into Christian service in many places over the years and through whose lives many have come to faith in Jesus. This is no place to exalt the ministry of the Keswick Convention, proud though I am to be part of that great movement. But it is significant to see how the message of holiness and surrender to Christ results in dedication to service. Mission and service are part and parcel of the Christian life that is being lived to the full. It would need a book in itself to record some of the stories of missionary service begun in the tent at Keswick. But something may be said and voices will be heard later in this book.

Keswick is more than the place of an individual call to service. Here at the Convention movements of missionary enterprise have begun which are of great significance for the Gospel in many parts of the world. It should not be surprising that where Christians from all over the world gather, the Lord gives a vision for the world. Sometimes slightly unusual things have begun at the Keswick Convention and most people associated with it today might not always be happy that the Moral Rearmament movement had its birth there when Buchman had a real vision of the Lord. But, year by year, we are reminded of more central and orthodox movements of the Spirit which had their birth at Keswick. We shall later be recording one or two of the facts which illustrate the beginnings of a movement of God in the world through the preaching of the Word in a Lakeland town in England.

Facts like these help to save Christians at Convention meetings from the awful danger of an introverted search for holiness. It is hardly possible to care too much about a holy life; it is very possible to be unhealthily inward-looking. One of the dangers of any gathering of Christians is that we forget the world around us and become self-centred in our thinking. Because of that, Christians have sometimes been led into extreme positions leading to claims of perfectionism which have not been lived out in practice. Or there is the similar danger that Christians who long for a closer walk with the Lord and new experiences of sanctification make extravagant claims. Church history is littered with manifestations of the 'second blessing' theory and many of these have stemmed from a

3

very genuine personal experience of the Lord which has been fossilised into some theory which in due course becomes like a chain round the necks of people who long to be the best for God. The challenge to mission and service is one of the healthiest ways of translating the call of God to a closer walk into positive action, and not just vague theorising or emotional experience.

It could be levelled at Keswick that sometimes we seem more concerned about individual holiness than about corporate holiness. But the second cannot exist without the first and this may well be an even greater danger in the church at large. In an age when social concern has rightly grown, some Christians imagine that if there is a response to the desperate social needs of our age, personal purity is almost incidental. For those who take the church and the world seriously there must always be an emphasis on the witness of the whole Christian community within the community of the world. Here the missionary emphasis helps to keep the balance and to send us out from a lovely fellowship of the people of God into the world to live out our new life in Christ. This is the balance of the New Testament. Our Lord could meet the disciples in the upper room in his risen presence and offer them his peace, but he would finish by sending them back into that world with a great challenge: 'As my Father has sent me, so I send you.'

Historically, wherever Christians have rediscovered the New Testament doctrine of holiness there has always followed a concern for the world. It is one of the great joys of the Keswick movement that it has seen the birth of similar Conventions throughout the world. It may seem incongruous to go to India, Africa and the Far East and to speak at 'Keswick Conventions'. I recollect having to try to explain to a rather bemused Korean television interviewer what the word 'Keswick' stood for in Christian terminology. Equally incongruously, I once sat on the edge of the desert in the north of Nigeria discussing fervently the projected visit of a Sudanese pastor to Keswick. Of all the historic places in England that he might visit, the only one that really appealed to him was Keswick, simply because the Christians who had led him to the Lord had heard their call to service at the Convention. So Keswick has become worldwide.

The birth of the Korean Keswick Convention recently is a marvellous example of how the Lord can use the challenge of the Convention to stimulate the ministry of the Word overseas. A Korean pastor studying in Europe came to Keswick as a guest a few years ago, was impressed by what he heard and saw, felt that there was a great need for it in his own country with their bursting congregations and their need for teaching. Within a year, Keswick in Korea was born and is now in excellent health. The greatest congregation to which I have ever preached, well over 100,000, was in the state of Kerala in South India at a Convention on similar lines to that of Keswick but outwardly so vastly different. In this way the message of the Keswick Convention has spread throughout the world and is a microcosm of the whole doctrine of the Body of Christ.

To those who have read the New Testament thoroughly, this should be no surprise. From day one, world conquest was in mind. Jesus sent the disciples with the audacious command to preach the gospel to the whole creation, and the church's birthday on the day of Pentecost saw people from many parts of the known world, including Rome, the centre of the world, hearing the message in their own tongues. That first strange miracle of speaking in tongues had a missionary message which none can deny. The great Keswick motto of 'all one in Christ Jesus' is not some marvellous ideal of the brotherhood of mankind. It is Paul's way of demonstrating what he had seen happening in his own ministry – people from all backgrounds finding their unity in Christ Jesus and the barriers of the world being broken down. He saw this as a very practical piece of theology and a remarkable preparation for the glory of heaven where people from all tribes and nations and peoples and tongues will gather around the throne of the Lamb (Revelation 5:9).

But that heavenly reality often seems distant and our more immediate objective is to achieve God's will on earth. Our Lord encouraged us to knit these two ideas together in the Lord's Prayer in the phrase 'Your will be done on earth as in heaven'. Christians should never apologise that they have in mind world domination, with the proviso that it is in the Spirit of Jesus and the conquest of love.

The missionary service which has this objective as its goal does not take place in a vacuum. One of the greatest contemporary challenges of our day would have been utterly unexpected a century ago. Militant Islam is hell-bent on seeking to win the world for its gospel. Not least Great Britain is in its sights as a possible place of conquest because of the apparent deadness of so much Christianity. Each year at Keswick we are reminded of the challenge of resurgent Islam. The Muslim world is on the attack and we must not be ashamed to carry the uniqueness of the message and person of Jesus to them. In a strange way this new move of Islam has at least killed stone dead the liberal concept that ultimately all religions are the same. No honest Muslim would be prepared to accept that and certainly no Christian who takes the name of Jesus seriously could live with it for a moment. We believe in the uniqueness of Jesus and with that assurance we must share him with others, not least those in the grip of Islam.

In the Communist world things are in a ferment. There is a strange transformation happening and he would be a bold prophet who would foretell what may happen within the next generation or two. Nonetheless Communism is still a powerful, world-conquering ideology. We may be able to rejoice that the gospel cannot be destroyed and that the church will grow even when persecuted under Communist regimes. The story of the church in China is a miracle in itself. The reality of a church growing when missionaries have had to leave should not surprise those who believe in the Holy Spirit and it may come as a salutary reminder that God is not bound by our ideas of church growth. But with all these encouragements we would be wise to remember how strong is the hold of Communism and how dedicated are its adherents.

I never tire of telling the story of being confronted as a young ordinand with an ardent Communist who came to our theological college to give us a taste of what Communism meant to one of its adherents. This young man had dedicated his life to the study of Communism in spite of having left school at fourteen and with no higher education. He was so dedicated to spreading this good news that he was prepared to manage on four hours' sleep a night in order to study and to give away a quarter of his income to the cause. After the meeting in discussion he gently chided some of us about our lack of enthusiasm. He maintained

7

that if only he could believe what we claimed we believe about God and Jesus and the Resurrection, he would be even more dedicated to that gospel. But with a shrug of his shoulders which I can still see across the years, he said, 'But I guess you guys do not really believe what you say you believe because Christians are not as dedicated to their gospel as we Communists are to ours.' There was nothing we could say and I believe that strange interview galvanised me to a concern for mission and service that has never altogether left me. How tragic if we are to play second fiddle to the evangelistic zeal of the Communist world with no true gospel to proclaim.

The cults are also on the march with Jehovah's Witnesses, Mormons and Moonies on the doorstep or at the street corner. Once more their zeal should condemn us even if we are not attracted to follow in their ways. Sometimes the ways of supposed evangelical Christians are not too attractive. One of the greatest disservices to modern mission and Christian service is the revelations of the American televangelists, as they are now called. By their blatant commercialism and with their claims of prosperity for all who will naively respond to their evangelistic call, they prostitute the glorious gospel of Jesus. It is hard not to believe that, wittingly or not, some of these men are perilously close to blasphemy. How brightly does Billy Graham and his team shine in that dark sky! If such travesties of the message and mission of the church have queered the pitch, we should be all the more eager to demonstrate what is a true evangelistic message and ministry. We must not sell the pass to the weird, pseudo-Christian ministries of our day.

These could be the days of the last great thrust in

world evangelism. I am very chary of undue melodrama in these matters and a biblical student will always beware of working out times and seasons. We must ever remember that these are in God's hands. But there is an Armageddon atmosphere about our day. It is not primarily theologians who are voicing prophecies about the end days. Often the most alarmist noises come from politicians, scientists and sociologists. As Christians we recognise that there is always a desperate urgency and we must match the hour with the message of hope. While yet there is time we must be about the Lord's business which always requires haste. In days of revival there were reports of Keswick meetings full of an atmosphere rarely seen nowadays, either there or anywhere in Christian conventions in this part of the world. Perhaps we need something of that atmosphere of excitement, of impending trauma. But above all we need a renewed impetus to proclaim the Kingdom before the return of the King.

My first book, tentatively written, was on the theme of the renewal of the local church, looking primarily at worship, preaching and mission. As a result of that book and comments about it I am even more convinced that one of the greatest failures of the church is along the line of mission. Even the word 'renewal' tends to become stylised, and people think in terms of new things happening in worship, new experiences in personal holiness or in the power of the Spirit, new avenues of spiritual adventure.

Many of these things may be very laudable and some of us do need quickening at this level. But I believe that we have become much too individualistic and much too introverted. The renewal in the life of the church must always be seen in a renewed vision

9

for world evangelism. When the Spirit first came he sent the disciples out on mission. The risen Lord Jesus made it clear that this was his priority and a renewed church will always be an outgoing church. We can fairly accurately evaluate the life of our church by the number of people being sent out in service and the involvement of church members in missions at home and abroad.

The last words of the risen Jesus are actually found in the book of the Revelation and not least in the solemn words to the seven churches of Asia. These particular churches have long ago disappeared off the face of the earth, destroyed not by the Muslim hordes coming in from outside but by lifelessness and death from within. The risen Jesus saw the danger even in those early days and in his warning to them comes a warning to the contemporary church.

He speaks to the church at Ephesus about its loss of first love – and how readily this can happen. We retain our orthodoxy and our zeal long after our love has gone and without love we shall never obey the divine commission.

The church at Smyrna was insignificant and earns the commendation of our Lord because it had been faithful even in the hour of testing, and that is a challenge to the church of today.

The churches at Pergamum and Thyatira are condemned because they have learned the art of compromise. The worldly spirit has entered in and the Christians have become very easily conformed to the world in order to earn prestige and popularity. How easy it is to rationalise our failure to dare to be different from the world around.

Sardis is a tragic church with a reputation of being alive but just about to die. Churches can live on the glories of the past when their effectiveness has long since gone.

Philadelphia is a church with an open door, with little personal power but with a great opportunity given by God. It could well be the type of many a church today, given a unique opportunity to reach out into a world of need and yet so aware of its lack of resources. It is good to be thrown back upon God.

Laodicea was a church which had lost its vision and lost its enthusiasm. In the process it receives the most scathing comment from our Lord. That apparently respectable church made Jesus sick, and doubtless it represents too many churches today. It is a lovely thought that to such a church come those marvellous words of Revelation 3:20 which have often been used effectively in evangelism. I remember it being quoted to me when I was at the point of conversion myself. It is valid at that point, but it is essentially not a word to an individual coming to faith but to a church which needs to allow the risen Jesus to enter in and to take over. To such a church and to many of these churches came the call to repent and that certainly is the call that our church needs to hear today. Without it there will be no renewed confidence in the gospel and when we consider our failure in mission we have much reason to repent.

When the disciples were challenged about their disobedience to the ecclesiastical authorities in Jerusalem by continuing to preach the gospel, they had to reply that they could do no other but speak. When Jeremiah felt that the message was too hot for him to pass on to others, he realised that it was like a fire in his bones and it had to come out. Sadly this is not always the reaction of the Christian church. It is very easy to find apparently good reason for not being overtly involved in evangelism and mission. Like the Jews after the exile who put the building of their own homes before the rebuilding of the Temple, we often cry, 'The time is not yet.'

Have you discovered a time which is absolutely perfect for evangelism? Have you ever discovered a perfect means of evangelism? Have you ever found any missionary service that is not tainted with some impure motivation? The devil loves to stop us doing the Lord's work in outreach and provides marvellous opportunities for us to discuss it and to wait for the perfect moment which he knows and we know will never come.

As one who has been involved in mission in my own church and in the wider work of the city and country, I recognise that there must be times when we concentrate on teaching and building up but it is equally true that this will go on the more effectively as we are reaching out together. We only grow by giving away and in any case if we honestly believe the wonder of the message that is ours, the great deposit handed down to us, we cannot possibly keep it to ourselves. Or if that motivation does not always excite us to action, our love for our Lord should mean a willing and joyful obedience. The Old Testament slave when offered liberation could always dedicate himself to willing slavery with the famous declaration: 'I love my master; I will not go out free.'

Christians are always in danger of moving into realms of hypocrisy. In our worship we proclaim the Lordship of Christ very fervently, particularly in the more devotional hymns and choruses of our day. Jesus often insisted that his Lordship was to issue not just in an act of submission or words of dedication, but in actions that prove we are his servants. In the vivid drama of the upper room narrative in John 13 where he washes the disciples' feet, he asks them to prove that he is their Lord by doing to others what he had done to them.

From the moment of his conversion the apostle Paul felt that his new allegiance to Christ symbolised by his bowing the knee on the Damascus road must be seen in taking the message to others. And so we have those haunting questions in Romans 10:14–15. 'But how are men to call upon him in whom they have not believed? And how are they to believe in him of whom they have never heard? And how are they to hear without a preacher? And how can men preach unless they are sent?'

I have never been able to escape that logic. Men can only call on the one in whom they have believed and they can only believe when they hear and they can only hear if someone speaks to them. How content are we to leave that to others?

But this obedience in mission must always be earthed in Scripture and not just become a superficial enthusiasm. Even mission can lose its biblical anchorage – hence the theme of this book, the ministry of the Keswick Convention and the belief that good biblical exposition should always result in response to the call. Such a foundation will save us from some of the failures of the past and the present. Mission is not just a social caring for the needy people of the world, nor is it a spreading of Western culture. In the past missions have failed on these and other levels and sometimes we are still reaping the tragic harvest.

It is vital to keep evangelism and social concern walking hand in hand. In one sense they are absolutely complementary. Our Lord himself in Matthew 25 makes it crystal clear that we are to serve him by caring for the sick and needy, the imprisoned and hungry. In a startling way he makes that the criterion of our eternal destiny. This is no elevation of salvation by works, but it is a reminder that faith without works is dead, and merely verbalising our love proves nothing except our skill at words. Always the evangelist should remind those who respond to the gospel that they prove their faith by care for others. Genuine faith will always issue in works. It is very instructive to study our Lord's words in the sermon on the mount in Matthew 7:21–23 where he speaks about the final day and the criteria which he will use. There is a condemnation of those who say 'Lord, Lord', but have not done the will of the Father. Their theology is right and their enthusiasms laudable but it is not enough. Equally in the next verse our Lord condemns those who speak of the activities they undertook in his name but whom he never knew personally.

As we seek to keep that balance we are also reminded that our Lord earlier in that sermon had spoken of Christians as salt and light (Matthew 5:13–16). The balance is clear yet again. Salt speaks of the gradual infiltration of Christian witness, often in quiet and unspectacular ways, giving taste and keeping from corruption. But light speaks of open witness which people can see. No Christian can ever avoid the need for an open testimony to Christ by action and by word. We should never let the salt metaphor hide us from the light nor the light from the salt. Holiness and evangelism are twin weapons of Christian testimony. What we are and what we say should go together.

Wherever there is teaching on the way of biblical holiness, whether at conventions like Keswick or in the ministry of the local church, there should always be a missionary presence and a contemporary presentation of the way of Christian service which matches the biblical exposition. Both should be earthed in Scripture and also in the world of today. Without the missionary dimension the theme of holiness can become introverted and pietistic. But the missionary challenge ought to be seen to be relevant to the world of today. The biblical message must be in a contemporary garb and equally the challenge to service. There is still a mentality of missions that lives in the world of 'From Greenland's icy mountains'. Equally there is a biblical exposition which is beautiful but ethereal and not relevant to the world in which we all have to live.

When both the biblical message and the missionary challenge are scripturally based and shot through with the life of today a real revolution can happen. It is the burden of this book to try to present the challenge of mission and service as a biblical priority and a contemporary reality. The theme is unchangeably true and uncomfortably challenging.

2: A Missionary God

God is a missionary-minded God. Therefore the people of God must have the same vision. From the very beginning of Scripture the God who is revealed cares for the whole world and puts man in charge of it. The great experiment of entrusting the created order to man made in his image is one of the great given facts of life. It is hard to conceive that we would ever have worked out this scenario. But here is the revealed truth that God has placed a being made like himself with whom he can have loving communion in charge of his world and responsible for it. Long before the story of the church begins, the story of the world is there in Scripture.

Genesis 1–11 are vital chapters if we are to understand the real world in which we live and our part in it. On the one hand it demonstrates man as made in the likeness of God, and at the same time as fallen from grace. It is the true story of man, the Jekyll and Hyde character that he is and ever has been. To try to understand the world and to change it without recognising sin is to be doomed to disaster before we begin. How many idealists have been broken on the rock of original sin which they have not been prepared to accept.

But happily the early chapters of Genesis not only

tell us about the real world. They also proclaim in advance the message of the gospel. Right there in Genesis 3:15 is the promise of the victory of the seed of woman over the serpent's seed. In the Garden of Eden the message of the Garden of Gethsemane is already being proclaimed. This is the gospel in its very origins, enshrined in the story of mankind from the beginning.

These early chapters demonstrate that God cares for the whole world and has a plan for it. He will call out his own people but only so that they might go back into his world to transform and redeem it. The message of salvation has a cosmic size. While it is true that the message of the good news is for the individual, it is equally true that it is for the whole world. That is the dimension of our gospel and of our God.

In these early chapters of Scripture we are reminded that sin will spiral and affect the whole of society. There is that chilling chapter 5 of Genesis where all the great men of the world are equally affected by the reality of death, apart from Enoch who had a relationship with God which broke through the death barrier. In different ways in these chapters we see that while sin is increasing, the grace of God is increasing all the more.

There is the story of God's covenant promises to Noah and then to Abraham. God takes the initiative, and as early as this in Scripture that marvellous word 'covenant' occurs. We cannot bargain with God but he can offer hope to us. For both Noah and Abraham the promise is not just for a particular person or family or race, but for the whole of mankind. God is at work providing a remedy, and yet equally in these chapters we see the inability of man to deal with the problem in his own way. The story of the tower of Babel in chapter 11 of Genesis is the beginning of the story of Babylon, which is the world set in defiance against God until in the book of the Revelation Babylon falls and the great choirs of heaven sing 'Alleluia'.

The tower of Babel speaks of man thrusting defiance into the face of God, making his own security, but it all falls pathetically short and God has the last word. Mercifully that last word has a wonderful echo in the New Testament. At the tower of Babel God divided the world because of its pride into different languages. On the day of Pentecost men and women from different parts of the world heard God's message in their own tongues. Pentecost has reversed Babel. In the babble of many voices in our world the people of God have, or should have, one voice with which to proclaim the great truth of God. The gospel unites the world while sin ever divides.

Always in Scripture the city of God is seen in contrast with the city of the world. Following the story of Babel, in Genesis 12 comes the beginning of the story of the church. Abraham's pilgrimage of faith is the beginning of church history. That pilgrimage is a picture of the life of the individual believer who responds to God's call and sets out in utter trust in his word. But it is more than that. It is the beginning of the story of God's people in the old and new dispensations. The promise to Abraham was not just for his own family but for all the families of the earth (Genesis 12:3). In that prototype of faith we note that the blessings of God are meant to be shared, and that more hinges on the individual's response to God than that individual can ever fully know. No act of faith is ever an isolated event.

The apostle Paul with his marvellous insight into the meaning of Old Testament Scripture will

19

demonstrate very clearly in Romans 4 and Galatians 3 that Abraham's offspring are all who share the faith of Abraham, whatever their race may be. The great theme of justification by faith and the unity of the church is already implicit here. In this way the story of Abraham inheriting the Promised Land can rightly be interpreted as a symbol of the people of God who have an inheritance not only in the glory to come but in a relationship with our Lord here and now (Ephesians 1:11–14 and 1 Peter 1:3–5). Our Lord himself commented that Abraham rejoiced to see his day (John 8:56), and perhaps that was fulfilled supremely in the dramatic events of Genesis 22 when Abraham was willing to offer his son Isaac upon the mountain as a supreme demonstration both of faith and of love. Many commentators have pointed out that this mountain top experience of Abraham with all its costliness was a very clear prefiguring of Calvary. The basic difference is that on Calvary God did not withhold the knife and his son was killed for our salvation. So at the heart of the Abraham story is the message of sacrifice which is ever the heart of the Christian gospel inspiring the church's mission.

The story of Moses continues the same emphasis of God calling out a people so that they might be his instruments in the world. The story of the deliverance from Egypt becomes in the Old Testament the theme of redemption and it is very significant that on the Mount of Transfiguration Moses and Elijah were discussing with Jesus his own 'exodus' (Luke 9:30–31). In very many ways that story reflects the life and ministry of the church. Deliverance was only through the shedding of the blood of the Passover lamb. The leading of the people of God was by the pillar of cloud and fire and the provision was through the manna and the water in the wilderness. All these speak of the life of the church and Paul in 1 Corinthians 10 can draw the analogies.

He can also point out that it is very possible to belong to the people of God outwardly and never finally to reach the Promised Land. Deliverance is not just out of sin, it is meant to be into the blessings of God. In the process the people of God become 'the congregation in the wilderness' (Acts 7:38). A congregation is a group of people called together through redemption and led by God. They are called together in order to be God's own people with a mission to the world. These are the terms of God's covenant relationship with his people in Exodus 19:5–6.

In the midst of those verses is the promise that the people of God are meant to be a kingdom of priests for the whole world since all the earth belongs to God. Just as Abraham was called out of the world to go back into it as a man with the blessings of God, so the people of God were called out of Egypt to become a nation to serve the world. The great rhythm of Christian service is already well established.

That rhythm speaks of going to God and going from God. Always the two must go hand in hand in balanced, wholesome, godly living. In the Old Testament it is seen in the balance, and, sadly, sometimes conflict between the priestly and the prophetic note. The priest would emphasise the going to God with sacrifice and prayer which could degenerate into mere ritual. The prophet would constantly proclaim the importance of speaking the word of God and living it out in holy behaviour day by day. Where the Jewish people in the Old Testament lost the vision of missionary service, they became either fossilised in merely formal religion or tragically proud of their own election. It led to a spirit of complacency which the prophets sought often in vain to destroy. God does not call us to himself for self-fulfilment, but only that we might glorify him and extend his Kingdom.

Even the extension of the Kingdom can degenerate and our Lord in Matthew 23:13–15 has to condemn the kind of proselytism which was a thousand miles removed from the spirit of true evangelism. Nor can we ever be complacent as Christians. Sometimes missionary endeavour has become mere religious proselytising and evangelism becomes an excuse for propagating our own particular views or churches. So much harm has been done by a sheep-stealing mentality which has presumed to call itself evangelism. At its worst this was a proselytising which Jesus had to condemn.

The true missionary concept of the Old Testament lay in a desire to spread the knowledge of God and his ways and also to demonstrate the attractive otherness of the people of God. In this way, holiness and outreach went hand in hand and this is the main thrust of this particular book. It has been the heart of the Keswick ministry. Holiness without evangelism can become unhealthy pietism. Evangelism without holiness can become very superficial indeed. Where the people of God lost their distinctive way of living they not only failed to further God's kingdom, they actually brought dishonour to his name. The prophet Ezekiel time and again has to complain that God's name is being blasphemed because of the way of life of the people who claim to belong to him.

It is salutary to note how often people turned in vain to Israel, seeking for a spiritual reality which had been lost. The attractiveness of the pure monotheism of Judaism was spoiled by the loss of life and vision.

The Ethiopian chancellor in Acts 8 was returning from Jerusalem disillusioned. He had gone looking for a faith that was real, and clearly had found no answer. Mercifully he was returning with the scroll of the prophet Isaiah, and even more mercifully he found by God's providence the man called Philip who had the courage and the insight to explain what Isaiah 53 really meant. From that Suffering Servant chapter he pointed the Ethiopian chancellor to Jesus and to Christian commitment. In that cameo we see the possibilities of missionary vision among the people of God. We have in our hands the word of God and we know the answer to man's needs as explained in the Scriptures. But we need to beware lest it becomes a dead book in the life of a dead church.

Much of the failure of Old Testament Israel lay in their desire to become like other nations and to reject their essential difference. Once Israel decided to become great politically, it lost out spiritually. In that spirit they decided they wanted a king like the other nations and Saul was given to them to satisfy their demands. In spite of the glory of King David's reign the rot had set in already and in the days of Solomon things went desperately wrong. A man greatly gifted by God became obsessed by his position and his grandeur. He became a king like the totalitarian despots of other nations, turning from God's ways and standards. At the point of its greatest political fame Israel was on the slippery slope to spiritual bankruptcy.

There is a parable for the church here. Sometimes in history it has been powerful and rich and utterly destitute like the church at Laodicea. We need to beware lest we seek after other greatnesses than the greatness of likeness to Jesus. Moses had reminded his people that God had called them not because they

23

were great but because they were the most insignificant of people, so that their boast would be not in themselves but in their God (Deuteronomy 7:7–8).

The tragedy of Solomon's reign was that instead of influencing the world for God, the Jewish nation had been influenced by the world away from godly standards. It is a parable of what may happen with the church set in the world. How easily the influence is in the wrong direction. We need to recapture the vision that Isaiah had in his great second chapter, seeing Jerusalem set as a centre of world domination. He saw nations all coming to the light which shines from his beloved Jerusalem. Micah has the same vision. But sadly both of them had to reflect immediately on the real world which was their Jerusalem and to start seeking a message which would cleanse and renew the nation. In the same way idealism in the church is not enough. We need to grapple with the realities of sin and to discover God's remedy for it.

Right through the prophetic ministry there is still the vision of the world which would turn to the God of Israel. Zechariah has this in abundance and he with the post-exilic ministry of hope could still see the prospect of a Jerusalem at the centre of influence in the world. In that remarkable prophecy we begin to see across the horizon the fulfilment in Jesus. In a very unusual way he dominates that book and Zechariah (a prophecy too much neglected) is frequently quoted in the New Testament in connection with Jesus. It was to fulfil one of Zechariah's prophecies that Jesus rode into Jerusalem on an ass claiming to be the Prince of Peace and bringing a message of peace not only to Jerusalem but to the nations. Zechariah 9:10 has that message of hope which straddles the Testaments.

It is one of the commonplaces of the Old Testament to portray the paradox of a nation which seeks to reach out to the world and yet maintain its exclusiveness. Both of these elements are necessary. There is the strand which has its symbol in the wall built by Nehemiah to keep the Jewish people pure. The whole of that book is to do with the theme of restoring and keeping a purified people, often with great militant activity. The wall symbolises separation from the world and has something of the sadness of the Berlin wall in our day. Yet we see Nehemiah's wall, unlike the Berlin wall, as being part of the providential plan of God. There could be no effective outreach until the Jewish people had been restored to purity of faith, till compromise had been destroyed.

The symbol of the other aspect of Judaism is in the story of Jonah where very reluctantly the prophet preaches to the enemy city of Nineveh and sees a massive repentance. It may have been that Jonah found it hard even to rejoice in that repentance and we note at the end of that book the most famous sulk in history when Jonah recognises what God has done. In spite of his missionary call being restored after early disobedience he still could not fully fathom the mind of God. He would have found it easier to understand the book of Nahum, which is purely a rejoicing at the fall of Babylon and has a picture of the whole world clapping their hands at such a fall. Nonetheless God used Jonah and the missionary message of Jonah is more important even than the miracle of his deliverance from the great fish.

The wall of Nehemiah and the mission of Jonah are two sides of the same coin. The church must keep itself holy and at the same time must burst out of any exclusivism and minister its message to a world of need.

Zechariah was a prophet who had the message and desperately wished to convey it. The vision of the man with the measuring line in his hand in his second chapter is very significant. The message is that the new Jerusalem must not be built within the confines of the old. The promise comes in verses 3–4 that 'Jerusalem shall be inhabited as villages without walls because of the multitude of men and cattle in it. For I will be to her a wall of fire round about, says the Lord, and I will be the glory within her.'

Here is a tremendous vision, not only for the Jewish nation in post-exilic days but for the Christian church in every day. It is all too easy to prefer the security of the past and the known. After all, Jerusalem had been very great and God had richly blessed her. But now there had to be the vision of expansion and also a trust in God's protection without the wall mentality. The vision was too much for the people of Zechariah's day and for days to come.

Even in the early church, converted Jewish Christians found it hard to believe that Gentiles could be accepted without first becoming Jews. They had learned to rejoice in the great Gentile influx into the fold but still preferred the security of Jewishness. Paul had to battle with Peter about this and the whole church had to wrestle with the revolutionary concept of what it means to be a new man in Christ.

Christians today are often guilty of sheltering behind the walls of past traditions. We find it hard to launch out into the unknown and trust God to protect us there. Like the disciples immediately after the resurrection but without the certainty of it, we huddle behind the shut doors of our church fellowship, keep ourselves cosy, and forget the challenge to go into all the world.

Such a venture in any generation is based on the sheer logic of the fact that in the truest sense all people are alike before God. It was hard for the Jews to accept that in Old Testament days, and the challenge of Amos 9:7 which placed the Ethiopians alongside the people of Israel and the migration of the Philistines alongside the deliverance of Israel from Egypt was disturbing stuff indeed. But Isaiah had a similar message, constantly in his later chapters seeing the ministry of the people of God as a light to reach out to the Gentile world. The picture of Isaiah 49:6 becomes a great New Testament inspiration. It is in Simeon's mind when he welcomes the infant Jesus and sees him as a light to the Gentiles as well as the glory of Israel. Paul will quote from it when he discovers, somewhat painfully, his rejection by his own people and yet the great openness within the Gentile world (Acts 13:46–48).

The concept of the people of God being light to the world demonstrates the double thrust of the witness in Scripture. Light speaks of truth and light speaks of holiness. Always the two must go together. The Jewish nation was given the privilege of knowing the truth about the One God and his demands upon people. The world needed to know that truth and be confronted with that life. Paul reminds us in Romans 9:1–5 of the great privilege of his own people and the tragedy that so often they failed to proclaim that truth and reflect that way of life. In world history much religion is divorced from holiness and it was a mark of the pure religion of the Old Testament that it linked the two together. 'Be ye holy for I am holy' is the great theme of the Old Testament Scriptures. It was the message of the prophets who drove home the priority of holy living in very practical terms.

27

The prophet Amos constantly called the people of his day to consistency of life in the way they conducted their business and ran their homes as well as in their worship. Some of his most stirring passages are on this theme, especially in chapter 5. But he was far from being a popular prophet and the priest Amaziah complained that he should be dismissed because he was disturbing society. All too easily, priestly ritual can go on without making any demands upon life. The message of the prophets, one of the greatest contributions of the Jewish race to the world, was to attack this blindness. The stage is being set for the New Testament doctrine of the balance between world vision and social concern. We must never put asunder that which God has joined together. Evangelistic outreach without social concern or social concern without evangelistic outreach are both demonstrations of an unhappy separation.

Most biblical commentators would agree that the story of Israel in the Old Testament merges into the new Israel of the church in the New Testament. There are inevitable areas of disagreement and there would be those who would want to make a plea for a continued interest in the historic Jewish nation and God's purposes for them. This is not the occasion to examine in depth this particular issue. But certainly the prophecy of Zechariah and Romans 9 – 11 would suggest that God has not finished with the Jewish people. But it would be sad if that truth were to obscure the even greater truth that the church is meant to be the successor to Israel. The great climax of Scripture in the book of the Revelation sees heaven as laid on the foundations of the twelve tribes of Israel and the twelve apostles. Surely the 144,000, so often misunderstood, speaks of the people of God in old and new dispensations and thousands of them gathered in the Kingdom of heaven. Therefore we are to see the challenge of the Old Testament as now coming directly to those of us who belong to the church of Jesus in which God's many promises are being fulfilled.

The missionary vision sits astride the divide between the Old Testament and the New Testament, not least because it is a message and ministry centred on Jesus himself. Our Lord would constantly quote the Old Testament to explain his own person and ministry. But it is surely significant that the themes he chooses are those of the Suffering Servant and the Son of Man rather than the more narrowly nationalistic Son of David. It is equally important that Jesus foresees his rejection by his own people and the Gentiles flocking into the kingdom of God (cf Matthew 21:42–43). Our Lord's personal vision will inevitably be a supreme stimulus to Christians. As we watch him at work and listen to him speaking we discover mission in a new dimension and yet so closely tied with the Old Testament ideal and inspiration.

3: The Son – On Service

Mission always involves senders and goers. Both are important in the Lord's economy. The two-way relationship in Christian mission is neglected at our peril.

I have been privileged for some years now to minister in a church where many people have been sent out into service, both in different parts of our country and abroad. In fact sometimes those called to service in tough contexts in Britain may well be even more deserving of prayer and support than some who have gone into fairly flourishing church contexts abroad. But there is no distinction and the service of commissioning as we dedicate people to this task is only the focal point of much continuing activity.

The pattern is set in the New Testament where the church in Antioch sent Paul and Barnabas on the first overseas missionary journey and there is a very interesting sequence of events as they report back constantly to their home church. The church in Antioch was fully involved in the sending out through prayer and fasting and was always there to welcome back, to hear and to pray.

With modern communications that relationship should be easier to maintain. It is staggering to conceive how Paul managed to keep the communications alive in his day. He was often sending out his minions such as Timothy and Titus to make contact with young churches born from his ministry. In our world with the possibility of tapes passing to and fro across the continents as well as telephone, radio and correspondence, there should be no difficulty in keeping that relationship alive. The goers are dependent upon the senders for so much support and the senders should be encouraged by the goers. Ultimately all of us should be in both camps at some stage.

One of the most moving words of commission on the lips of Jesus is in this realm of sending out. In John 20:21 the risen Jesus says to the still dispirited disciples 'As the Father has sent me even so I send you.' It is easy to dwell on the final command but in fact it is all based on the great awareness that our Lord himself had been sent. Indeed the way in which he sends us out in love is parallel with the way in which he was sent out by the Father. This does not suggest any unwilling going but a joyful participation in the Father's will. In his ministry Jesus was constantly aware of having been sent on mission and from time to time there comes a nostalgic awareness of how much Jesus left behind. Coming down from the transfiguration mount he wonders how long he must go on being with the disciples with all their unbelief. Perhaps on the mountain he had felt himself near to the Father in a very special way and would very much love to have been home again.

Paul senses the wonder of this in his famous verses at the beginning of Philippians 2 or in 2 Corinthians 8:9 where he contrasts the riches that Jesus left behind with the humility and poverty of his life on earth. It was not so much that he left opulence for rags, but rather that he left that close, intimate

32

relationship with the Father to come to earth, to be separated in one sense from the Father and even more on the cross to have to bear the moment when God forsook him as he bore the sins of the world. Not only did the rich become poor but the righteous became a sinner in the sight of God for the sake of our salvation. It was costly obedience. For Jesus to be sent was not irksome but it meant the cross, willingly and sacrificially borne.

Jesus seems to have been aware of this sense of mission certainly from the age of twelve. In that unique insight into his young life we see Jesus in the Temple, aware that he must be about his father's business. He is thinking not of apprentice carpentry but of a readiness to complete the mission for which his heavenly father had sent him. All the ritual of the temple would remind him of the final sacrifice that he had to make. It is impossible to conceive how that was understood in the mind of the adolescent Jesus. But we do know that as soon as his ministry begins in earnest he is aware that he has come on a special mission. This mission is not primarily to heal or even to preach, although preaching will have a great priority. In Mark's Gospel when Peter and the others seek to find Jesus to engage him in more healing ministry he insists that he must move on to the next town to preach, 'for that is why I came' (Mark 1:38). In fact he came primarily to make a gospel that others would preach, but his own preaching of the Kingdom was a significant preparation.

What a blueprint this is of real mission. We may never be sent to win man's salvation but we certainly are constantly being sent to proclaim the good news and all ancillary ministries must ever be subservient to that.

Throughout his life this sense of mission dominates the thinking of Jesus. He will talk in terms of 'my hour' and all the more as he nears Jerusalem and Calvary. His face will be set towards Jerusalem for this is the ultimate goal of his life on earth. There is a very moving passage in Luke 12:50 where Jesus, speaking of his cross as a baptism, can cry, 'I have a baptism to be baptised with and how I am constrained until it is accomplished.' The word 'constrained' speaks of that inward compulsion put there by God to send Jesus to the climax of his mission. The verb is used of the armies of Rome encircling Jerusalem or of the crowds who pushed Jesus, and Paul will use it in another moving passage where he talks about the love of Christ compelling us (2 Corinthians 5:14). In every way the ministry of Jesus sets the pattern for mission which should ever be in front of the Christian servant.

There is a uniqueness in our Lord's ministry which can never be repeated. When he spoke in terms of his hour, always referring to the climactic moment of his sacrifice on the cross, he was speaking in terms which can only dimly be echoed by the Christian. There is no way in which we can ever atone for the sins of others. But we are encouraged by our Lord to take up our cross and follow him. Just as our Lord set his face to go to Jerusalem and would not be deflected from it, so the apostle Paul was determined to get to his Jerusalem. St Luke sees the parallel very clearly as he writes the two volumes of his great story. So we may have our hour and we may be conscious that God has called us to a definite purpose which will involve sacrifice and maybe suffering. Paul had a great longing to know Christ and the power of his resurrection, and the fellowship of his suffering (Philippians 3:10).

There can be no short cut to the power except through the fellowship, no way of enjoying the resurrection without sharing the sufferings.

That uniqueness of Jesus extends to his very life, the incarnate Son of God, living out his life on earth. Once more we cannot imitate Jesus and we would be foolish to imagine that what he was able to do through his incarnate being we can expect to do ourselves. But we are called to live out the Christian message as well as proclaim it. In one sense we are meant to incarnate the very life of the gospel in our society.

John in his writings very clearly compares the incarnation of the Son of God and the incarnation of the love of God through the people of God. In John 1:18 he points out that nobody has ever seen God at any time but Jesus the Son of God has made him known. Then in 1 John 4:12, using the same pattern of words, he reminds us that again nobody has ever seen God but if we love one another, God dwells in us and his love is perfected in us. To hold those two together is a very thrilling experience. What John really says is that by the love of God seen through the people of God, we reflect Jesus. In that sense there is a continuing incarnation of the Son of God in the life of the church. That is why Christian mission after the pattern of Jesus is often best seen through a community. I would always want to argue that the most effective evangelism is done through the life of the local church. Mission through the local church is not only a proclamation but an exhibition. The church for better or for worse is the greatest audio-visual of all time.

Uniqueness is also a characteristic of the miracles of Jesus. These signs and wonders, which John indicates in his gospel are meant to lead us to faith and new life, mark the very special ministry of our Lord. The very fact of a God-man would have been a miracle in itself, even if there had been no virgin birth by which it began. The resurrection of Jesus is a supreme miracle and therefore the Christian faith is absolutely based on the miraculous. No Christian should ever seek to walk on water or to change water into wine. But we do have the promise of Jesus in John 14:12 that his works we may do and we may even expect greater works.

Commentators and Christians have often argued about that verse. Very few would really expect that in any sense we can do greater miracles in kind than Jesus did. It seems to point to the wonder of the fact that the reality to which those signs pointed is even more effectively seen in the life of the church than in the life of Jesus. You could argue that Pentecost was the first fulfilment of John 14:12. With the thousands added to the kingdom in one day the church was seeing more obvious success than all the ministry of Jesus in a numerical sense. Throughout the history of the church we have seen this verse being gloriously fulfilled.

But we may equally expect that the miraculous will happen. Recent years have reminded us that we dare not assume that the gifts of the Spirit died with the apostolic age and that miracles are only a thing to expect in the days of Jesus. We need some caution when dealing with signs and wonders but it is equally wrong to rule them out altogether. So in the mission of the church there will be primarily a proclamation, leading to the greatest miracle of all – the demonstration of the Spirit in power in changed lives. Sometimes that will be undergirded and spotlighted by signs and wonders which demonstrate that we are dealing with the same God who worked through Jesus in transforming power.

If our Lord in all these ways was unique, we are still called to follow in his pattern of life and ministry. Paul exhorts us in Philippians 2:5 to have the mind of Christ. This has many ramifications but it certainly does speak of following his pattern of ministry and outreach. That pattern began with the Jewish people. Jesus would always give them priority, and in the dramatic dialogue with the Syrophoenician woman Jesus apparently cruelly had to demonstrate that the children must be fed before the dogs. In using a gentle form of the word often used for Gentiles our Lord was drawing out the remarkable faith of this Gentile person. He would not withhold his blessings from those who did not belong to the Jewish race but he wanted clearly to demonstrate that he came to the Jews first. When he sent the disciples out he would send them first of all to the lost sheep of the house of Israel (Matthew 10:6).

Certainly the apostle Paul never forgot that lesson and in each place he would start with the synagogue and seek to convince the Jews of Jesus' Messiahship. Almost inevitably he was rejected but he still kept the same pattern, the Jew first and then the Gentile (Romans 1:16).

There is I believe in this very significant fact a challenge to evangelism. We must start where we are in the church of Jesus reaching people on the periphery, seeking to bring spiritual renewal to those who have religious affiliation, and then begin to move outwards. In that way we consolidate the work, we provide a church that is ready to receive, and we gear the whole family of God into evangelism. This lies behind our Lord's famous last words in Acts 1:8 that the power of the Spirit was to enable the early church to witness to the ends of the earth but starting in Jerusalem. If I do not care for the people who live next door I certainly will have no effective ministry in the Third World. I must begin in my Jerusalem. But Jerusalem will always remain not the goal, but only the starting point of mission. Jesus himself could never limit his ministry of loving care and teaching to one group of people. He met every kind of need in every kind of person. Inevitably therefore the widening of the ministry began and the pattern was set for the whole church.

Not surprisingly, St Luke is particularly interested in this ministry since he himself was a Gentile convert. In his Gospel we see many illustrations of our Lord reaching the despised people of his day. For example, he would take time to minister to children, there will be many manifestations of his care for women in his ministry, there will be a special stress on the work amongst the outcasts of his day whether the person with leprosy or the hated tax-collector. It is all of a piece that St Luke records our Lord's story of the Good Samaritan, where the hero of the story is from a rejected community while the villains are Priest and Levite, exalted members of the religious Jewish community. Equally in St Luke's narrative we read that the only leprosy victim who returned to give thanks after healing was a Samaritan. So Jesus broke down the barriers. His love embraced all.

There is a particularly vivid juxtaposition in Luke 18 and 19 where Jesus, busily moving towards the goal of his ministry in Jerusalem, meets Bartimaeus, a blind beggar, and is very willing to stop to heal and help him. In the very next incident he deliberately goes out of his way to call Zacchaeus to himself, a man equally rejected because of his position. Jesus cared for the up-and-outs as well as the down-and-outs for he recognised the need of all. Following the

Zacchaeus incident, Jesus makes the definitive comment about the thrust of his ministry. 'For the Son of man came to seek and to save the lost.' Similar words recur in the fifteenth chapter of Luke where Jesus tells the story of the Lost Sheep, the Lost Coin and the Lost Son. He is eager to explain to cynical Pharisees that his Father is a God who goes out of his way to reach the lost. That is his characteristic, and it should be the characteristic of all who name his Name.

In a similar analogy Jesus could liken himself to a doctor whose ministry centres on those who know that they are sick. He cannot help those who are unwilling to admit their need of help. Therefore it is not surprising that the ministry of Jesus always had a double edge to it. It is seen particularly vividly in some of the dialogues around the miracles of Jesus. For example, in the ninth chapter of John we have the vivid drama of the man who was born blind being made to see by Jesus and then becoming involved in a desperate wrangle with the religious leaders of his day. To be healed by Jesus is not always the pathway to peace. Sometimes in the short term it is easier to stay in an unregenerate condition. As a result of the dialogue, Jesus has to comment in John 9:39 that he had come into the world to bring things to a head. He was a man always bringing a crisis and in that crisis some who were blind would come to see and some who thought they saw would go into greater blindness. It is impossible to be confronted by Jesus without moving in one direction or another.

This is always the challenge of mission and service . No Christian following in the path of Jesus can expect not to find rejection and hurt as well as acceptance and joy. It is a superficial reading of the Christian message to imagine that those who preach it will carry everything before them. If our Lord's ministry could be explained in terms of the parable of the soils with their differing responses how much more that will be true of every servant of his. Some of our Lord's controversies centred around the fact that he healed on the Sabbath day. It almost seems as if Jesus quite deliberately brought about this confrontation because he wanted people to see the two differing kinds of religion, longing that the Pharisees might understand that the Sabbath was given for man's wholeness. But a legalistic view all too often prevailed. Following Jesus may mean that our confrontation will not be with the irreligious but with those whose religion has blinded them to the truth of the gospel and whose doctrinaire attitude will not allow them the liberty of the Spirit.

Faith which leads to life comes from a response to the truth proclaimed in the teaching of Jesus and in the miracles which undergird that teaching. So John in his Gospel selects some of the signs which Jesus gave in order to bring people to faith and through faith to life (John 20:31). There is no evidence in the New Testament nor indeed in church history that signs and wonders of themselves lead to a massive response of faith. Often indeed the reverse is true and Jesus will sigh about his generation which demanded signs and would not see the signs that were in front of them. In John 9 the Pharisees were not convinced by the evidence which they could not gainsay. They were only driven into greater opposition.

So Jesus in his very telling story of the rich man and Lazarus is not only giving us an insight into eternal realities and the divisions beyond the grave, he is also pointing out that where people do not believe the word of God no sign will ever convince them. There is a sting in the tail of that story and in Luke 16:31 we read, 'If they do not hear Moses and the prophets, neither will they be convinced if some one should rise from the dead.' We may at first almost want to doubt that firm word of Jesus, but experience will remind us that when Jesus himself rose from the dead his enemies were not, by that token, convinced although they could find no argument against it.

Always Jesus caused divisions and always there were people ready to hear and believe. We may expect the same kind of response when we follow Jesus. In his ministry the greatest miracle of all was that of changed lives to which all the signs pointed. Ultimately lives could only be changed through his climactic work on the Cross. Hence when the Greeks wished to see him Jesus did not indulge in a miracle or profound teaching ministry. He just spoke about himself as a grain of wheat going to die to bear fruit. The harvest could not come until that moment of self-sacrifice on the Cross. Nonetheless in his life on earth he did revolutionise many lives. At the end of John chapter 2 we are reminded that he knew what was in man and therefore had a unique ability to help man. The next two chapters of John illustrate that perfectly. Immediately in John 3 Jesus meets a religious man Nicodemus and in some startling dialogue he challenges him to be born anew or born from above. And then in the next chapter Jesus unexpectedly meets the exact opposite of a person, a prostitute woman from Samaria with whom no person of Nicodemus's ilk would even have been speaking. With that woman Jesus had a very significant religious conversation. He did indeed call her to repentance by reminding her of her moral failures, but he also deigned to discuss with her the wonder of God being spirit and truth.

It is interesting to ponder how we would have dealt with those two different personalities. Most of us would have called the woman at the well to be born anew and would have discussed spiritual issues with the religious man. Jesus knew that a man however religious needed spiritual rebirth, and a person however far gone in disobedience to God's moral commands, could have a spiritual dimension. The call of Jesus is to challenge people wherever they are to that spiritual transformation he alone can bring. We may not naturally have the insight of Jesus. We do not by nature know what is in man and no amount of psychological training will enable us to have that wisdom. But we may have by the Spirit wisdom from on high, and learning from Jesus we may be able to bring a message which can transform any person. This is ultimately the concern of all Christian mission.

Whether the offer is along the lines of the rather abrupt challenge to Nicodemus to be born spiritually, or the more gentle offer to the woman at the well of a never-ending supply of inward satisfaction, the message must always be that the priority need is in the realm of the spirit. Sometimes in Christian service we have been so busily engaged in all the ancillary ministries of care and social compassion that we have almost felt that this was enough. This certainly we must do, but we must not neglect that which is even more significant and has eternal results.

This can be seen vividly in our Lord's ministry. A paralysed man is brought to him for healing and he first of all offers forgiveness, since he sees this as a basic need without which healing will be almost incidental. A similar man is encountered in John chapter 5. When this man is healed Jesus deliberately finds him and urges him not to go on sinning, lest something worse happen to him. In our age so obsessed by physical health it is hard to conceive anything worse than 38 years of sickness. But Jesus clearly believes that the results of sin are greater than the results of disease. But always we keep the balance, since Jesus did heal both these men, and we must never apologise for the pastoral caring ministry we exercise in Christian service.

In keeping this balance there is sometimes conflict which can only finally be resolved as we watch our Lord at work as the greatest missionary and servant of all time. There is the remarkable verbal similarity in our Lord's words to two very different women recorded in Luke's Gospel. Identical words are used in Luke 7:50 and 8:48 'Your faith has saved you; go in peace.' On the first occasion Jesus is speaking to a woman of doubtful reputation who has demonstrated her love for Jesus by anointing him and he has proclaimed the wonder of forgiveness to her. It stood out in dramatic contrast with the lack of courtesy given to him by his Pharisaic host. The woman in chapter 8 was a person with a debilitating disease who touched the fringe of our Lord's garment and was healed. Jesus wanted to give her something greater than mere physical healing, and also to strengthen her with assurance. He makes her stand out and testify to her healing. Then he can speak the words of assurance. Both these women were sent into peace.

Both had been 'made whole'. One needed no physical healing but only the wonder of the healing which comes through forgiveness. The other, undoubtedly a sinner, was not so much in need of forgiveness as of physical relief. In both cases it was an act of faith that latched on to the power of our Lord bringing wholeness and sending into peace.

It is also a reminder of our Lord's concern not just to give immediate help but for a new way of life to flow from it. All mission deals with felt needs with an awareness that our Lord in his sovereignty can meet each one, although not necessarily in the way we would desire or envisage. But also there is the confidence that there are needs way beyond those of the moment. And in the new relationship with our Lord in the Spirit there is abiding peace, that shalom which only Christ can ultimately give.

From the earliest days of his ministry Jesus was preparing his disciples to continue his work. He sets a very significant pattern for all Christian ministry. We need constantly to look at our church structures to see whether or not we are adequately training others to take on the leadership in our own community and extend it outside the community. Jesus knew the limitations of his time and therefore prepared his disciples to spread the good news while he was still alive and to take up his mantle after his death, resurrection and ascension.

As early as Mark chapter 3 we get the story of the twelve being called to him. The purpose of that calling was to be with him and then to be sent out. It was vital that they learned primarily by being with Jesus. He would give constant teaching but it was also a matter of watching the Master at work. We do well to copy that, both with Jesus and by following those who are following him in leadership. Those who were called to be disciples spending time with him were also called to be apostles, sent out to continue his ministry.

There were times when Jesus took that training further and used the disciples in the miracles. Most enlightening is the use of the disciples in taking out the bread and the fish to the five thousand. They became agents of his power. On more than one occasion Peter, James and John were specially invited to share the more intimate moments with our Lord. This is partly a reminder of his humanity and the need for someone to share crisis moments with him, especially in the Garden of Gethsemane. But it is also yet another part of his training of leaders in ministry, watching him and learning from him. Then come the moments when he sends out the twelve and later the seventy to continue his mission of preaching and healing.

But all this is before Calvary and before Pentecost. In one sense the disciples could only fully carry on the work of Jesus when that work had come to its completion in the sacrifice of the Cross. The risen Jesus could then send his disciples out with the good news of what he himself had already done through Calvary. So in Luke 24:47 our Lord tells the disciples that they should preach repentance and forgiveness of sins to all nations. Our Lord had now completed his work and made the gospel to be proclaimed. There is in our Lord's determination to come to that climactic moment a pattern for our own ministry. Very clearly St Luke sees our Lord's journey to Jerusalem as the inspiration of Paul's journey to Jerusalem and to Rome. Our Lord himself gives this insight when in John 12:20–26 in the incident of the Greeks coming to see him, Jesus talks in terms of a grain of wheat dying to bear fruit, thus speaking of his own forthcoming death. Then he will drive home the parallel and insist that Christians who serve and follow him must be ready to lose their own life for the sake of Jesus and the Gospel. We too have our hour and must have the same absolute determination of Jesus to fulfil God's purpose for our lives.

Having seen the pattern of our Lord's mission and ministry we are the better able to understand the words of the risen Lord to his disciples when he left them in charge. It is a solemn thought that the church is in the world as the continuing representative and presence of Jesus. That lay behind the moving account in John 20 of Jesus meeting with the risen disciples and sending them out as the Father had sent him. He would breathe on them in anticipation of Pentecost. Without the empowering Spirit we can never obey the commands of that great commission which still remains the church's manifesto. But it makes a lot of sense to listen to the terms of that commission, and then to realise the impossibility of doing it in our own strength. Then there is the excitement of the possibility of doing it in the strength which the one who commissions us also gives us in his Spirit.

4: The Great Commission

'The Great Commission' – these words have been traditionally written across the words of Jesus in Matthew 28 verses 16–20 as a dynamic title. Our Lord brings the ultimate in challenge to service and missionary enterprise of every kind. It is a gloriously triumphant passage, both end and beginning. Here the story of Jesus merges into the story of the church. As St Luke will remind us at the beginning of his second volume, the Acts of the Apostles, the work of the church is continuing the story of all that Jesus began to do and to teach. The daring call to the eleven disciples becomes mind-blowing when you think of the implications. But nothing less would fit with the audacious claims of Jesus to have ultimate authority in heaven and on earth, including world dominion.

Authority is a word often used in the Gospels to speak of the ministry of Jesus in his teaching, in his healing and in his call to men and women. The church should also be characterised by authority, not an authority of its own but under the lordship of Christ. All too often the church is ignored because it does not speak with any clearly authoritative voice. Jesus claims lordship. This is a theological truth which undergirds all Christian experience. There can be no genuine Christianity without acknowledging Jesus as

Lord (1 Corinthians 12:3). It is also the truth which lies at the birth of all Christian experience. Jesus is Lord whatever our response may be to him. The challenge to the disciples was to work out the implication of that truth in their lives. We must constantly ask ourselves: do we take the lordship of Jesus seriously?

This triumphant ending to the Gospel balances Matthew's introduction with its story of the wise men at the feet of the infant Jesus. That remarkable event symbolised the world under the authority of Christ. Now he calls his followers to make that symbol real throughout the world. So the Gospel closes with this open-ended call and we are still living in the light of it.

Earlier in the narrative the disciples had been sent out exclusively 'to the lost sheep of the house of Israel' (chapter 10 verse 5). We may never go back to that exclusivism, and the joy of the Gospel is that no longer is it for any one race or people. But it is a reminder that the whole world begins at home. So in Acts 1:8 Jesus will insist that the Spirit-filled disciples start their witnessing in Jerusalem. Every Christian should gauge the reality of his or her commitment to Jesus by the desire to be a witness in our home context. Charity always begins at home but if it ends there it is certainly not of God.

Jesus demands to be Lord not only in name but in reality. If he is our Lord then we may never keep such revolutionary news to ourselves. Paul, who loved his own people and longed for their salvation, never lost sight of the goal of a whole world acknowledging Jesus as Lord. Romans chapter 10 should be constantly open before Christians seeking to discover God's will for their lives. It poses some unanswerable questions concerning those who cannot call upon the Lord because they have not believed in him, and who do not believe in him because they have never heard. Somewhere somebody should be hearing that call to be sent.

For these disciples about to be launched on the greatest mission in world history it begins with a symbolic bowing of the knee. It all happens in the frontier situation of Galilee, always seen as almost a no-man's land between genuine Israel and the Gentile world (cf. Isaiah 9:1–2). Christians should always be those who live on the frontier, both geographically and socially. We are never called to exist in some spiritual ghetto, even though we desperately need to move into our church fellowships for strength to go out into the world. But even those church doors should be open. Jesus had to come in his risen power through shut doors to chase the disciples out into the world. We are called to live on the interface between the church and the world. In us and in our fellowship there should be a glorious overlap of the ages.

But Galilee was not only a frontier situation, it was also the place of obedience. Jesus had told them to wait for him there (verse 10), and always a Christian will find that the place of the next call is where we are obedient to the last one. It is ever a matter of one step at a time in Christian guidance and obedience. They went to Galilee not knowing what the next step would be, just as Abraham in Genesis 12 stepped out in faith, not knowing where he was going. We always go with sealed instructions and we never have laid out before us the whole pattern of our future life. We walk by faith and not by sight.

In that place of obedience we are honestly told that some had doubts. It was all too good to be true and it is heartening to know that even with those doubts the Lord could use his disciples. It is often by going in faith with a residuum of doubt that we actually discover how real he is and our doubts begin to evaporate. For these men the evidence of the risen Lord took time to become a strong conviction. For most of us throughout our Christian pilgrimage there will be the cry of the father in the Gospel narrative, 'Lord, I believe; help my unbelief.'

But if some doubted, the main element of this encounter was a bowed knee in worship. It was a new moment for the disciples with their newly-risen Lord. In a similar way the blind man who had been healed in John 9:38 bowed the knee in acknowledgement of Jesus as Lord and in worship of him. We live in a day when worship has been resurrected in all its joy and importance. But there is always the danger of empty worship and meaningless words. To worship God is to tell him what he is worth and in that very act of bowing the knee we are dedicating ourselves to go out in service.

Alongside the bowed knee goes the open ear. Worship is at its best when we are learning new things so that we might worship the more. Teaching is at the heart of church activity and is all too often at a premium. There is almost a feeling abroad today that too much learning might spoil the relationship with our Lord and lessen our love. Ignorance is not bliss for the Christian. These disciples, before being commissioned, were being taught afresh. During the forty days with the risen Lord they had been reminded of great truths of Scripture and had been given teaching now enshrined in the New Testament. This goes on right to the end. The new truth they were learning here was the authority of Jesus in all the world and spreading into eternity. To learn such a truth is to be committed to its proclamation.

In the New Testament, churches that came alive were always churches that were well instructed. The great missionary-sending church at Antioch had a whole year of being taught the truth by Paul and Barnabas. It is not surprising that such a church could not contain the message to itself. The story can be read in Acts 11:19 ff. This message of complete authority in Jesus is set over against the claims of Satan in Luke 4:6 that he has authority over this world. In one sense Satan spoke the truth but he is ultimately under the sovereignty of God and the final authority is in Jesus. In that spirit we go out into the contest between Satan and our Lord for effective domination of the world. Scripture calls Satan 'the prince of this world'. Our task is to wrest that world from his grasp, confident that Jesus has already won the victory. Satan need not be in control. But the battle is real. Satan has his own missionaries, and we do not serve in a vacuum but in the midst of cosmic conflict.

There is a sense in which our Lord's claims in this passage are only possible because he has gone through Calvary. He has won this place of authority by his obedience unto death. The world could not be won without the victory gained at the Cross. He foreshadowed this when in John 12, confronted by a group of Greeks wanting to see him, he spoke in terms of being a grain of wheat falling into the ground and dying. This was a message they had to hear. It was not enough just to watch some great miracle of his power. Jesus knew that the world could not be won by any short cut. This was the battle that he had fought out with Satan in the wilderness. The bread of life to feed the world is always broken bread. If that is true of Jesus, it is equally true of the Christian. We are called to follow in his footsteps. We too must learn what it is to be broken bread and grains of wheat dying so that through us the message of Jesus can be heard and become credible. In Paul's vivid language in 2 Corinthians 5:14 'The love of Christ controls us, because we are convinced that one has died for all; therefore all have died. And he died for all, that those who live might live no longer for themselves but for him who for their sake died and was raised.' The awareness of the greatness of God's love in the self-giving of Jesus is the constant motivation for Christian service and sacrifice.

Convinced of the truth of our Lord's authority, we shall gladly obey him. Such obedience will result in lives being changed in their direction and quality. No more do we seek to discover what we would like to do with our lives. We do not seek our own fulfilment but are always available, at his disposal, since he is Lord and has authority over us. The Christian disciple then has the responsibility to proclaim the lordship of Jesus to others and to demand the allegiance of others. We must beware of a wrong kind of authoritarianism which is not of the Spirit of Jesus. But equally we must beware that in a desire to seem to be loving we do not lose all sense of authority in our message. We must never be ashamed to proclaim that Jesus is Lord.

The apparently insignificant words of Scripture are often most important. Jesus opens his command with the link word 'therefore'. In the light of his authority and the disciples' worship the call is to go out, to bring in and to build up. It is the constant pattern of Scripture that the way we live depends upon what we believe and the more we believe the greater the challenge to behave. Regular reading of scripture is a dangerous occupation because God has a habit of speaking clearly through it. All of us who are preachers and teachers know how consistently God calls people to a new level of living and to new spheres of service through his Word. It is one of the testimonies to the inspiration and authority of Scripture that still God uses it to call people in contemporary situations. Every one of us must be listening to that 'therefore'.

In the first place it is a call from Jesus to go out. In the Christian life there is a beautiful rhythm of coming and going. It is vital that we come into the place of quiet to pray and into the place of fellowship to worship. It is dangerous if we stay there. There is a very significant chapter in St Luke's Gospel where vividly the comings and goings of Christians are brought together. In Luke 10:25–37 the story of the Good Samaritan is told to challenge a lawyer who loved to discuss to be doing something, and indeed it ends with the command, 'Go and do likewise.'

But there is the opposite danger. In the delightful cameo of Martha and Mary and Jesus in verses 38–42 the challenge is to the activist Martha to stop being so busy and to start following Mary and make time to listen. There is the possibility that some who are active in going need to stop and come into the presence of God. But equally some of us hide our failure to obey under a cloak of religiosity. We are very busy in worship and fellowship. How often have I come across groups that excuse themselves from evangelism because they are all too busy getting to know each other in an intimate fellowship. Satan is very subtle.

With the Lord's challenge to go comes a very clear goal and the goal is nothing less than all nations. Because of what Jesus did on the cross there is a universality about the message. He died for all men and therefore no lesser goal will satisfy.

Not only has it a geographical connotation but it is a reminder that every part of society and every race should be reached. The book of the Revelation depicts every nation and race worshipping the Lamb, and we must constantly be on our guard lest we keep the Gospel to ourselves and deny its universal validity by re-creating barriers that have been broken down in Christ Jesus. In Acts 1:8 our Lord demonstrates that this goal may be reached in different stages with his challenge to start in Jerusalem and then through Judea and Samaria go to the ends of the earth. We may not reach our goal until we have dared to start at home. Evangelism and missionary service are two sides of the same coin.

There is an inevitable sacrifice implicit in the going out. Like Abraham in the Old Testament we are often more aware of what we are leaving behind than that to which we are going. It may be a matter of leaving behind a town or country that we know and love for foreign places. It may be leaving the security of a job in which we have our assured place, in order to move into service where the future is unknown and the provision unsure.

But we are not only challenged to go out, we are to bring in. Jesus does not send out his disciples merely to be salt and light, although that is a very high and holy calling. We shall not be very effective at bringing people into the kingdom if our lives do not mirror something of the love and the purity of Jesus. But our Lord is thinking in terms of world dominion. He does not envisage Christians being a gentle influence for good. He is not in the business of syncretism where all religions are saying the same thing with different voices. He envisages the church growing numerically as well as spiritually. The call is to make disciples. This means more than making converts, although that is the beginning. Those who turn to Christ will then become disciples and be built up in the faith of Christ. Then they in turn go out in service and so the lovely multiplying process continues. It is the theme of 2 Timothy 2:2, which has often been a key text in days of Christian growth of a biblical pattern. Our task is to pass on what we have heard to faithful men who in turn will teach others also. In that sequence there is no end.

Making disciples is a call to do more than care for people's material and physical needs. Scripture is adamant that we may not preach to those who are in desperate bodily or social need without caring for those needs. The apostle James has some straight words on that score. But we must never be content with helping men and women to find hope in this world. Man does not live by bread alone and the church must not be ashamed to proclaim it, even if in the process it is misunderstood.

Our Lord himself cared for people and ministered to their immediate needs, but his miracles of healing were always signs of something deeper. After he had fed the five thousand he would argue with the crowds, complaining that they were more interested in the physical sign than they were in the message it had to convey. They were challenged not to spend their time on the meat which perished but on that which endured to eternal life (John 6:27).

Good Christian missionary service will always wed together physical needs and spiritual. In an age of horrendous crises with millions starving it is tempting almost to neglect the creation of Bible Schools to instruct Christian leaders, or the provision of Christian literature to build them up in the faith. But we must insist that Christian stewardship will always keep the balance. The call of Jesus was not primarily to feed the hungry but to make disciples.

The call to baptise the new disciples underlines the need for open commitment with its message of a living relationship with the Trinity. We need to proclaim the caring love of our Creator Father, the willing sacrifice of the Saviour Son, and the enabling power of the Holy Spirit in the individual's life and in the fellowship of the church. The new Christian becomes part of that community with those resources. Here is the distinctively Christian sacrament and a reminder in a day of militant religions of many kinds that the Christian, without losing humility and graciousness, is meant to be openly proud of his Lord and Saviour.

Indeed, with all its imperfections, he is equally proud to be a member of the family of the church of Jesus. From the beginning Christians were called into a fellowship of believers. Those who go out in missionary service go out from their fellowship with the assurance of the prayers of that fellowship and their greatest desire is to serve or help to create a similar fellowship within the same overall church of Jesus Christ. One of the distinctive miracles of the Spirit's work is to create new branches of that church family. The most searching definition of the church is found in the beginning of Paul's letter to the Corinthians where he speaks of 'The church of God which is at Corinth, those sanctified in Christ Jesus, called to be saints, together with all those who in every place, call on the name of our Lord Jesus Christ, both their Lord and ours'. To be part of that community is the greatest privilege in the world and with it comes a solemn responsibility to introduce others to its fellowship.

But our Lord's commission does not end with the challenge to make disciples and baptise. He urges them to a ministry of teaching, a teaching which is based upon the words of Jesus himself. So it was in the church at Antioch, when new life had come through the dynamic witness of anonymous Christians, that Barnabas and Paul spent a whole year teaching the church and building them up in the faith so that they might stand and expand. Paul always majored on the need for an edified church. In his long debate about the gifts of the Spirit in 1 Corinthians 12 and 14, he almost monotonously keeps on reminding them that the greatest gift of all is to edify or build up the church.

This could well be the most crying need of the world church. It is certainly the greatest need here in Britain and, from my experience, in many parts of the world. Because Satan has his minions with false teaching, it is vital that Christians are strong in their knowledge of Scripture and deeply founded in the faith. A high priority must ever be given to the quality of the teaching in our churches, in the ministry given to children and young people. Where there is a famine of the Word of God, it is even more disastrous than a famine of material bread. It is not so easy to portray the urgent need of people dying spiritually but somehow the message must get through. Jesus was anxious that young Christians should be taught and instructed. That kind of investment is a long-term one that ultimately will mean a stronger and richer Christian witness in the world.

To face the great commission is the most humbling thing in the world. No person in his or her own strength can even begin to cope with it. It was almost ludicrous to imagine that these early disciples could even begin to turn the world upside down but they did, and the Acts of the Apostles is the beginning of that great story. But first we must recognise our utter inability in our own resources.

Throughout Scripture this is the pattern. Moses quails at the prospect of leading his people out when he has been humbled by a lifetime's experience and then he is reminded that his God is the great I AM. Joshua, following Moses, feels completely inadequate to walk in the footsteps of such a great man but is promised the presence of God, the God who was with Moses and would be with Joshua. Gideon, when he is called to service in days of national crisis, admits that he is utterly feeble but the same promise of God's presence comes to him. Isaiah in the temple hears the call to service, but is only able to obey when he has been cleansed and empowered. The disciples at the end of the Gospel narrative, huddled in the upper room because of fear, hear the challenge to be sent in the same way in which the Father sent Jesus, but that could only happen when Jesus breathed on them and they received the Holy Spirit.

It is always vital to balance together the two great truths of our inability and his ability. In John 15:5 we are reminded that without Christ we can do nothing and in Philippians 4:13 that in Christ we can do all things. So the Christian will ever live in the tension of fear and confidence. There is fear because of an awareness of the immensity of the task and the inadequacy of resources within ourselves and confidence because we know that our God is able.

So our Lord in these verses makes the promise which ends this Gospel so triumphantly and echoes across the centuries with the testimony of saints down the years. 'Lo I am with you always, to the close of the age.' It is vital to remember that this promise can only be claimed by those who obey. In the simple terms of Scripture you cannot have the 'lo' without the 'go'. There is no easy promise of our Lord's presence if we sit in our spiritual armchairs viewing the world and discussing matters. There is certainly no awareness of his presence if we disobey his commands. But if we risk in faith, whether in terms of going out in service or daring to witness or starting a new career trustfully, we may claim the promise. It is a promise for every day. Literally our Lord promises to be with the disciples 'all the days'. That would include days of apparent success and days of despairing failure. It will be seen in the story of the Acts of the Apostles as these same disciples trusted the Lord, followed his pattern, and discovered that he was able both to guide and to strengthen them to achieve the impossible.

But the promise of Jesus is not just for all the days, it has a climax. Jesus promises to be with them 'to the close of the age'. Christians must ever bear in mind the assurance that Jesus will return, and with it the solemn challenge to reach people while yet there is time. Our Lord in Matthew 24 speaks a good deal about the certainty of his return and declares that this will be when the Gospel has been preached throughout the whole world (Matthew 24:14). Therefore Christians will always engage in world evangelism in the light of that day of return. Matthew 24 is full of warnings about the danger of not watching and not being faithful. It is a call to every Christian servant to live in the light of the imminence of our Lord coming back.

That sense of urgency has often been lost. In the

days in which we live, full of impending fears of Armageddon, the Christian should re-capture this sense of urgency. In a day of revival a great Scottish preacher said to his friend, the famous Murray McCheyne, 'Brother, let us hurry.' He was not speaking of an engagement to be fulfilled or a train to be caught. He was speaking of the need to get on with the job of preaching and evangelising before it was too late. That ministry in evangelism will always include the caring for the needy which is a proof of our obedience. So in Matthew 25 when the theme of our Lord's return continues, it ends with that very solemn picture of the Son of Man on his throne separating the sheep from the goats. The test is what they have done to the least of these, the brethren of Jesus.

As the hour could well be getting close to midnight and the day is dawning we must all afresh take seriously this commission and the lordship of Jesus. There is no time to lose.

5: Carry on Christians

The Acts of the Apostles is a very significant document in the story of Christian mission and service. Coming from the pen of Luke this is not surprising. His own story is full of uncertainty and romance in the true sense of that word. We can make an identikit of him from the few references to him in the Apostles and by following the narrative of his second volume. His gospel also demonstrates something of his character and his faithfulness as a historian.

He was a Gentile almost certainly, a medical man who may well have appeared suddenly in the story in the Acts of the Apostles acting in his medical capacity with the constantly ailing apostle Paul. Certainly the 'we' passages begin in Acts 16:10 at the time of Paul's vision of a man of Macedonia which ended a series of closed doors. It may be that one of the reasons for closed doors was the apostle's health and Luke may well have appeared on the scene to meet that need. But much is lost in uncertainty. It is equally interesting to conjecture where Luke discovered all his information. One answer may lie in the fact that he was around in Caesarea for two years while Paul was in prison. No doubt as a faithful historian he used that opportunity to the full. We know from the introduction to his gospel that he was a man who, with good medical precision, studied the facts and sifted them carefully.

In his two-volume narrative Luke sees the Acts as the continuing story of Jesus. At the beginning of the book he refers to 'all that Jesus began to do and teach' and that refers to the whole story of the Gospel. We may therefore see the Acts as the ministry of Jesus continuing through his disciples. Our Lord himself gave that impression in the narrative in the Upper Room when he assured the disciples that they would be rejected as he was rejected. The servant would follow in the footsteps of the Master. But that continuing ministry could not happen without the power of the Holy Spirit. It is very significant that the disciples with all the intellectual conviction that Jesus had risen from the dead could not begin to preach on the first Easter Day. They had to wait until Pentecost, so that there was inward enabling to match the conviction of the external truth of the resurrection.

So the final word of Jesus to his disciples in Acts 1:8 is a reminder both of the possibility of power for service and also the priority ministry of the Spirit in people's lives. It is not possible to witness without power and it is not possible to enjoy the Spirit without being called to witness. He can be the uncomfortable Comforter to those who want experience without challenge.

It has often been commented that Act 1:8 is the index of the book. The ever widening pattern of witness is from Jerusalem through Judea, through Samaria, to the ends of the earth. Quite deliberately Luke ends his story when Paul is in Rome and preaching the Gospel unhindered. Rome as the centre of the world was the fulfillment of our Lord's promise for that generation. The great unfinished task is always with the church. Each generation must start from its Jerusalem and reach out to the ends of the earth in that day. There can never be a missionary enterprise which completes the task. Only our Lord's return will do that.

Yet this verse is much more than an index to the contents of one particular book. It is the pattern for all Christian service. We receive power only through the Spirit and that power enables us to be witnesses. The word speaks of public testimony but even more of costly commitment in service. It is the martyr word and it reminds us that from the beginning some had to make their witness by the shedding of their blood. For all of us Christian witness can never be an optional extra nor a leisure pursuit. It is the total commitment of our lives.

It is revealing to see how the pattern of Acts 1:8 is fulfilled in the story. The moving out from Jerusalem only begins because of the persecution around the person of Stephen. In God's providential way he thrusts out his people, often not of their own volition but in his sovereignty and sometimes through much pain and suffering. Yet the story of that movement began on the Day of Pentecost with the giving of the Spirit. Many people have commented that the book ought to be called The Acts of the Spirit rather than The Acts of the Apostles but both titles will do. Clearly the Spirit is in charge. Without his empowering there would be no witness and he it is who opens and shuts doors as the story evolves. At the same time the apostles are instruments in his hand and it is the fulfilment of our Lord's command which is also a promise in John 15:26–27 with its double witness of the apostles and the Spirit himself. In every generation the Spirit has his own way of moving the church. But we are never treated as puppets and he still needs his 'apostles'.

Pentecost is more the birthday of the church than a blueprint for the church. It is always vital to remember that we may expect every promise about the Spirit and we must obey every command about the Spirit. But we may not expect that he will always work in the same way as he did in the Acts or even in periods of revival in history. It is fatal to try to cage and confine the Spirit.

But there is much in Pentecost for us to ponder as we consider the challenge of mission and service. The audio-visual of that moment was significant with the sound of the wind and the sight of tongues of fire. Throughout Scripture the Spirit is seen in terms of wind, whether in the vision of Ezekiel in chapter 37 or our Lord's promise to Nicodemus in John chapter 3.

Equally when God is at work it is seen as fire, as at Mount Sinai or Mount Carmel with Moses and Elijah. There is about both these elements a note of mystery. We certainly do not control the wind nor can we produce the fire. But we must be ready to be moved by the wind and ready to be set on fire by God's Spirit. Equally the picture is of a great sheet of flame dividing upon each of the apostles. The Holy Spirit makes us one and yet indwells us personally. Christian service is not a lonely exercise, doing our own thing for the Lord. It is the corporate ministry of the church, although sometimes it may ask for a lonely response and even a lonely ministry within that total work of the church. When Peter got up to preach, inspired by that Holy Spirit, he was the mouthpiece and yet he did stand up with the eleven (Acts 2:14) and this symbolises the whole church and ministry. So in Act 4:33 we are reminded that 'with great power the apostles gave their testimony to the resurrection of the Lord Jesus and great grace was upon them all'. The church itself preaches although it will have its interpreters in preachers and teachers.

Already on the Day of Pentecost in Jerusalem the missionary enterprise has begun. There is a great roll-call of the nations represented, including 'visitors from Rome'. There was great potential in that gathering at Pentecost, and we must ever interpret this phenomenon for our day. The world has become a very small place and often gathered in one particular spot is a whole world ministry in embryo. With vision we could see the potential as people from overseas flock into Great Britain and the missionary challenge is on our doorstep.

It is impossible to estimate just how much flowed from that first moving of the Spirit in Jerusalem. We certainly know it began by the phenomenon of speaking in tongues, probably different from the similar gift spoken of in 1 Corinthians, because here people heard them speak in their own tongues and understood. The miracle made people ask the question, 'What does this mean?' Some in cynicism saw it as mere drunkenness but Peter took the opportunity of starting from that point and proclaiming Jesus. It is always the work of the Spirit to point to Jesus and whatever the Spirit does in our life is to focus on our Lord. So on the Day of Pentecost the division of the world at the tower of Babel was gloriously reversed. There at Babel God in judgement divided people. Now at Pentecost God in mercy unites them. The only hope for unity in our world is where people are one in Christ and in the Spirit.

From Peter's sermon we may learn just what must be the content of all Christian proclamation. Peter himself with his new-found courage was a demonstration of the power of the Spirit. How different from the man who could not acknowledge Jesus before a serving maid. He was also inspired to focus his ministry not on the Spirit but on Jesus, and the whole sermon breathes the wonder of our Lord. He speaks of Jesus of Nazareth, of Calvary, of the empty tomb, in glory and at work now. It was a bold proclamation of truth. It challenged individuals to respond, making it clear that the death of Jesus was the responsibility of those who heard. It all mounts to the climax of verse 36 where he wants people to know that this Jesus is truly Lord and Christ. It is a sermon awaiting a response. Christian service will always home in on the person of Jesus and drive home the relevance of the gospel to the individual.

Only the Spirit can bring conviction of personal sin and that happened very markedly on the Day of Pentecost. But Peter was able to give the answer when conscience was quickened. We may not usurp the Spirit's prerogative but we must be ready for him to be at work. Peter's offer in Acts 2:38 is a double offer of forgiveness for the past and the gift of the Spirit for the present and the future. Alongside the double offer is a double challenge, to repent and be baptised with the obvious assumption that this speaks of turning to Christ in faith (cf. Acts 3:19). It is a call to an inward response with an outward, open confession in baptism.

It may be significant that Peter saw no problem in baptising there and then. We do need sometimes to look at our very careful preparation courses before we allow people to be baptised or to make their profession in other ways where there has been infant baptism. But equally it was vital that these people should be nurtured in the faith, and the famous Jerusalem quadrilateral in Acts 2:42 is ever the yardstick by which we judge all our nurturing of young Christians. There must be the apostles' teaching to build them in the truth, fellowship to encourage, the breaking of bread and worship for inspiration, and prayers as we bring everything to God. We may not assume that every single person of the 3,000 baptised on the Day of Pentecost went on triumphantly. Indeed everything in the New Testament experience suggests the opposite. But there is a lovely picture of a communalism which rebukes our over-individualism in the church of Jesus.

The early church saw many evidences of the Spirit at work through signs and wonders, not least the dramatic healing of the lame man in chapter 3 which became the springboard for yet further outreach and evangelism. There will always be differing views as to how much we may continue to expect these signs and wonders. But certainly we must never limit the power of the Spirit and where God works in very signal ways in people's lives we must be eager to drive home the message from those occasions. But we need always to remember that the signs are not complete in themselves, otherwise they would not be signs. They are called to point to the greater truth of a new life in Jesus which he offers.

There is evidence that the Christian church in Jerusalem became content. It took the dramatic visionary Stephen, called in the first place to be a deacon and a helper, to arouse ferment that led to his own martyrdom, the persecution of the church and the throwing out of Christians to fulfil God's pattern. There is great drama in the fact that Saul was very much an instigator of the death of Stephen, and yet it

67

was Stephen's death which began the revolution in his life. It pricked his conscience, disturbed his theology and led eventually to his own glorious conversion. Nothing in the history of the church is more significant for missionary endeavour than the conversion of Saul. When we ask therefore about God's sovereign plans for a young man like Stephen, we remember that out of his death came life for Saul. We must always rest content that God is sovereign over our lives, and he can use the death of Stephen as much as he can use the healing of the lame man. A theology that does not allow for both as part of God's purpose will always be misguided and dangerous.

In the next wave of Christian expansion it is enlightening to see how God is at work at both ends of the equation. In Acts 8 he brings Philip out of a revival work in Samaria to meet a solitary Ethiopian chancellor on the desert road to lead him to Christ and possibly be the beginning of a great church. In Acts 9 he takes the insignificant Ananias and uses him to bring Saul fully into the kingdom and to baptise him. In Acts 10 and 11, with some trouble he persuades Peter to go into the home of Cornelius and preach the gospel, leading to a moving of the Spirit in that Gentile home and the beginning of a great movement of non-Jews into the kingdom of God. It may be significant that apart from eager Philip, in all the stories the Christian is less flexible than the non-Christian. Ananias argued with God's decision and Peter was very reluctant to follow. It may well be that in the world there are many waiting for Christians to have the courage to step out in faith. The same Lord who moves us to take the good news will be moving at the other end in the lives of people to receive it.

The story of Peter and Cornelius is very much a test

case. Because of the importance of the occasion God gives Peter a very special vision. It is instructive to see in Scripture how sparing God is with his visions but they are always meaningful. The vision of the sheet and the unclean animals was to remind Peter of the basic truth that 'what God has cleansed you must not call common' (Acts 10:15). It was not primarily a matter of the laws of hygiene and the traditional Jewish food laws. It was to be interpreted in the light of Gentiles already there longing for a Jewish Christian to bring them the food of life.

Eventually Peter gets the message, crosses the Rubicon and goes into a Gentile home preaching the Gospel. The Holy Spirit sets his seal upon this revolutionary moment which breaks down ancient barriers and the household of Cornelius is gloriously converted. Peter must face the logic in Acts 10:47 and baptise those who already possess the Holy Spirit. The message is enunciated in Acts 11:17. 'If then God gave the same gift to them as he gave to us when we believed in the Lord Jesus Christ, who was I that I could withstand God?' God had worked and the church slowly got the message.

Peter himself was under pressure to go back on this revolutionary commitment. We find a moment in Antioch, recorded in Galatians chapter 2, where Peter and Paul have an eyeball-to-eyeball confrontation on this whole issue. It was hard to live with this great truth, but in the sight of God it did not matter now whether you were Jew or Gentile. All are one in Christ Jesus.

Paul will later proclaim that message in Galatians 3:28, and over the years this has become the motto of the Keswick Convention. It is not primarily to do with the breaking down of denominational differences, important though that is. It is a reminder that at the foot of the Cross and in the light of all that God has done for us in Jesus, all other differences matter not at all.

It would take some time before the early church could live with this great truth and sadly many of us still find it hard to accept. It would be easy to draw up a list of the barriers that still divide Christians and the number of secondary matters that have become basic and fundamental. For example, there are those who believe that it is not possible to be a true Christian without being totally immersed in baptism. There are those who believe you cannot be a genuine Christian without being confirmed. There are those who wrongly affirm that you cannot be a true Christian without speaking in tongues. All these are adding to the simple faith of the Gospel. Whatever the merits of these issues, they cannot become fundamental. That flood gate was opened when Peter preached in the home of Cornelius and God accepted a Gentile believer on the same ground as every circumcised Jewish believer.

If missionary enterprise was already in embryo in Cornelius's home it goes a stage further in birth in the great story of Saul's conversion in Acts 9. It is not just the story of a man who was changed right round, and it justifies three accounts in the narrow compass of the book of the Acts. Implicit in Saul's conversion is the birth of a missionary and right at the very beginning of his Christian life service he is called to be a chosen instrument of the Lord to witness to Gentiles and to suffer (Acts 9:15–16).

It is also an important lesson to learn that Paul's conversion story was in two halves. On the Damascus road he met the Lord personally and was transformed.

In the Damascus home through the gracious ministration of Ananias he was brought into the family of the church and the corporate side of his conversion was accomplished. To become a Christian inevitably means to be involved in the life of the church. To be converted means inevitably to be committed to service. That service will not be merely a matter of witness by word, but a readiness to suffer after the pattern of Christ.

The early years of Paul's ministry drive home yet another lesson. He immediately becomes a witness in Damascus and is immediately in danger of his life. From now on Paul will never be allowed to rest. Barnabas graciously trusts him, unlike many of the Christians in Jerusalem who feel that he is a traitor spying out the land. Paul's very obvious belief that he had particular gifts to reach fellow Jews was shattered by their refusal to accept him and then he has to spend a considerable time back at his native Tarsus working out his Gospel, witnessing to Gentiles and, even in apparent frustration, being prepared for his unique ministry. So in the Old Testament Moses had a long wait after his first vigorous attempt to lead his people. For forty years he was being prepared in the desert for his task. We are all too often in a desperate hurry. It may have been in those months of waiting that Paul began to work out something of the tension of seeking to reach his own fellow-men and yet being called to a wider world and rejoicing in the breaking down of the barriers. Romans 9 to 11 may well have been there in his mind during those days, at least in embryo.

Then comes Paul's first great ministry in Antioch where the word 'Christian' was born. That church in Acts 11 and 13 gives a vivid illustration of a missionary-minded church. In the first place it was a church which lived through the testimony of anonymous Christians. We have no idea who first witnessed there, but we do know that they were people scattered against their will because of the persecution around Stephen. The Lord has his own sovereign ways of spreading the Gospel, and it is more often through suffering than through great success. Where ordinary Christians are prepared to speak of their faith, that is missionary service. It is unlikely that God would call a person to some great task if he or she had no vision for the ordinary ministry on the doorstep.

Then the church at Antioch was a church which learned the Gospel. Barnabas came to see what was going on. With his normal graciousness he was able to see God at work but also to recognise the superficiality of much of that faith. Enthusiasm is never enough to form the basis of a thriving Christian community. So for a year Paul and Barnabas taught the Christians and out of that strengthened church came renewed vigour and the first overseas missionary venture.

Not least the Antioch church had very practical concerns of love. When they learned of famine in Jerusalem apparently spontaneously they formed the first Christian Aid venture, thus early teaching us that the Christian enterprise will always balance the needs of the body and of the spirit.

It is not surprising that from this dynamic church in Antioch with all its vision came the first overseas missionary enterprise. But the occasion in Acts 13 is full of deep significance. The call came to the whole church at worship. Often the Bible is silent when incidentals do not matter. We may be curious to know how the Holy Spirit did speak to them but we are not told and we are not meant to be told. But we do know that here was a church on the right wavelength to receive the message, and it is an indictment of many of our churches that we do not hear the Spirit speaking in this kind of way because there is not the commitment to prayer which this involves. It suggests that it was the normal worship of the church, not some special occasion to find out the future. But it is also significant that after the word had come they went back to fasting and prayer to make doubly sure.

Even more remarkable is the fact that the Lord's call was to send out not two of their young and eager Christians but their respected and cherished leaders Barnabas and Saul. How many churches would so gladly have seconded their leadership for such a venture of faith? But the whole church was involved and through the laying on of hands symbolised that involvement.

When the first missionary journey is over Barnabas and Saul return to the church at Antioch in chapter 14:27 and tell them what has happened. Again it is significant that they do not come back with the stories of suffering which could have abounded nor even the stories of their exploits which were fascinating. Primarily they told of what God had been doing and how he had opened a door of faith. Happy the church which has this kind of every-member involvement in missionary service. Senders are just as significant as goers.

The story of the first missionary journey is full of important guidance for all who are concerned with mission and service. For example they begin in Cyprus, an island which had very obvious connections with Barnabas and his family besides being geographically adjacent. The Spirit's guidance very often comes through natural and normal channels. We must never despise the ordinary and the obvious. Equally in

Cyprus they go straight to the cities and straight to the people in positions of importance. We must never despise the rural ministry nor should we ever become a movement which is only interested in leadership. But all too often the reverse has been true and we have failed to plant the Gospel at the heart of cities, and we have failed to reach people whose position makes them potentially great men and women for God.

Paul always goes first to the Jewish synagogue and continues that pattern however much he is rejected. He has no doubt that the Jews with all their background knowledge of Scripture must first hear. But he moves to the Gentiles with alacrity and finds there a ready harvest. The parallel can certainly be drawn today. Evangelism will often begin with those who have church background, some residuum of faith. Often the greatest opposition will come from these quarters. Then we must be ready to go out daringly into a world with so little contact with God and yet so often desperately needing the message.

Not least we may learn from this journey the confidence that Paul has in preaching the Word and in the ministry of argument. He will match the message to the ability of the congregation to receive it. In the synagogue he is full of Old Testament allusion; when he is confronted by pagans he refers more to creation. But Paul believes in reaching people's hearts and lives through their minds. It is possible to be too cerebral. It is much more likely in these days that Christians have lost confidence in speaking out intelligently the message of God and arguing it home to the minds of unbelievers.

Even a cursory reading of these chapters in Acts makes those of us who want to serve the Lord today feel acutely uncomfortable. For most of us life is easy and pleasantly predictable. For Paul and his group anything could happen at any time. It was never dull but it was certainly never safe. To read in 2 Corinthians 11 Paul's fairly prosaic account of the costs of service is to make us ask serious questions about our readiness to sacrifice for the Lord. Missionary contexts will vary and we are not asked to be foolish martyrs. But for Paul it was often a matter of life and death. That may have led to his apparent harshness in not taking John Mark on the second missionary journey because he had turned back for some unexplained reason on the first expedition. Paul recognised that there was a certain toughness needed in Christian service and ultimately it will ever be so.

This comes out particularly movingly when Paul, after attempts on his life, must go back to follow up Christians in places of danger to encourage them. With all his toughness there was a great vulnerability about Paul. He often bared his soul and he was gentle with young Christians. But when he goes back in Acts 14:21–23, to follow up those young Christians in that first missionary journey he emphasises to them that entrance into the Kingdom is through many tribulations.

We must shun like the plague the kind of teaching which offers us ease and prosperity. The New Testament picture is the exact opposite. If we follow Jesus we may expect constant pressure, but with it the peace and the joy of the Lord.

With the success of that first overseas mission there came a problem which had to be faced once and for all. It was the problem of the open door, of which Acts 14:27 speaks, through which many Gentile believers were passing who had no knowledge of the Old Testament Scriptures and no adherence to Jewish moral standards. The problem then, as now, was: What is the bottom line?

Of course it is essential that people who become Christians should follow the clearly defined moral standards of Scripture and there can be no compromise there. But it should be equally clear that many of the cultural pre-suppositions that go with the Christian Gospel are not essential. So the great Council of Jerusalem in Acts 15 wrestled with the problem, coming out with a statement that came not just from their deliberations but from a revelation of the Holy Spirit. It insisted that in things essential there should be unity, that in things non-essential there should be liberty, and that in all things there should be charity.

We need to work out that formula in every age. For us it is not a problem of circumcision or food laws but it is a matter of culture and habit, of language and life-styles, dress and behaviour. Harm has been done in trying to sell a package of Western culture with the Gospel of Jesus. These early battles in Christian mission still have to be fought and won in every generation. How vital to keep the unity of the Spirit and yet have within it the great diversity of different traditions and backgrounds. That is the richness of the Christian faith which we must cherish at all times.

We can also learn much from the strategy of mission in the Acts of the Apostles. Paul clearly had a plan and was very determined in following through that plan. But he was also very sensitive to the guidance of the Spirit. This balance comes out beautifully in Acts 16 and the call into Europe. Clearly Paul had a plan for the evangelisation of Asia Minor but doors kept shutting. Acts 16:6–10 is a most important paragraph. We are not told exactly how the Spirit shut doors but Paul was always ready to accept such a decision. Having been obedient to the negatives Paul was then ready when the positive vision of the man of Macedonia came. Immediately there was action. We need to learn to wait when God demands it of us. But equally we must never hang back and deliberate when the call is clear.

Paul's early ministry in Europe is fascinating, with the very different typical responses in Philippi of a religious lady ready to open to the Gospel, of a demon-possessed girl who needed deliverance, of a down-to-earth jailer who could be transformed by the power of God and a man who spoke the Word of God. There is a whole wealth of missionary vision in that chapter. In each case as Paul went around Europe we see opposition, and Paul's willingness to face it when necessary and to move on when doors were shut. There is the parenthesis in Athens where Paul intellectually debates with those who scoff at the whole concept of an incarnate Son of God and a message of resurrection. He can demonstrate how vulnerable he is when he goes to Corinth and feels desperately lonely, needing a special vision of the Lord to encourage him to go on in that evil city. And in Ephesus there is a door of tremendous opportunity but also a place of great conflict.

There is always the healthy balance of Paul getting on with the job in a pragmatic spirituality and yet at the same time the sense that here was a man who knew that he was going places. This comes out as he sets out on his epic journey to Rome via Jerusalem, beginning in Acts 19:21 with a sense of the Spirit's guidance and a determination in that Spirit to get to his Jerusalem and Rome, not unlike Jesus with his face to his Jerusalem. Some of us Christians are so busy with the immediate that we have no sense of strategy or vision. Others spend their time with drawing boards and planning sessions but rarely get anything done. How we need that healthy balance of the apostle who had to get on with the job but who longed to see the world won for Christ.

Paul's journey to Jerusalem and then to Rome is a whole book in itself. But some things stand out very clearly. Paul's attitude towards the attempt of others to deflect him from his purpose is interesting. Even prophetic words he will politely ignore, since he is so sure of God's will for his life. It is a salutary reminder that we must always listen to what others say with great respect, but at the same time we must have our own mind. There is a danger that sometimes because of due deference to the authority of others, we lose out on our independent judgement which is our prerogative in the Spirit.

What stands out supremely in this last journey to Rome is Paul's sense of God's overruling. Instead of it being a matter of weeks, it became years, including two years confined in Caesarea, and when Paul gets to Rome he arrives not as a preacher but as a prisoner. Nonetheless he can write in Philippians 1:12 that everything worked out for the furtherance of the gospel. Because of his position in Rome as a prisoner he was able to reach the praetorian guard as they were chained to him. There is no better example of a captive audience! Such men would never have gone to hear Paul preach in the synagogue. Or again because of Paul's imprisonment it made the whole subject of the gospel a matter of public notoriety. Sometimes people talked about Jesus because of Paul in terms which were antagonistic to Paul. But he had learned to be happy, providing Christ was preached, whatever might be the motivation (Philippians 1:15–18).

St Luke in writing the Acts of the Apostles sees Paul in Rome preaching unhindered as the climax of the unfinished task for that age. Clearly the unfinished task remains until the day of our Lord's return. We are to seek to fulfil the great commission and to follow through the pattern set in Acts 1:8 for our own age. We still have a challenge in our own Jerusalem and in the neighbourhood. Not least we can see the ends of the earth in a very different light today but still awaiting the good news of Jesus.

It may well be that Paul did not finish his days in Rome. There is evidence that his great desire to go on to Spain, expressed in Romans 15:23–24, may well have been fulfilled but of that we have no definite record. We do know that here was a man so dedicated to the Gospel that he would go flat out until the Lord blew the final whistle. We need more of his ilk to face the challenge of the unfinished task today.

6: To the Church – With Love

There is a unique quality about the Gospels and the Acts which always leaves a gentle question mark in our minds. How far may we expect God to work today as he did through our Lord and by his Spirit in those unique early days of the church?

Some have no problems and assume that it will always be like that and only our lack of faith spoils it. Others eager for dispensationalism would suggest that we may not expect this at all; these events marked something which can never be repeated.

A careful examination of those books suggests that we should be expecting God to be at work in ways very similar to those in the Gospels and the Acts. But alongside that was the proviso that Jesus was of course unique and that Pentecost and all that followed was the birthday of the church. Yet John 14:12 keeps on haunting us with its promise of the works that Jesus did and even greater works. Therefore there should be a divine discontent about the level of the church as it so often appears, without embracing some of the wilder claims that surround the churches today.

With all that in mind we turn to the letters of the New Testament on the theme of mission and service with an utter certainty that this is for us. Here are Paul, Peter, John and others giving to the churches a blueprint of what God expects of them. Here is a challenge for the next generation and here we can rest content that it is a word for us today. It is a pattern of Paul's letters in particular that there is a balance between theology and conduct, between belief and behaviour. Paul builds up the doctrinal section and then, often with the little word 'therefore', works out some of the implications of those great truths. Good behaviour follows from good belief. If we get our doctrine wrong we shall get our ethics wrong. A generation or two ago some theologians and church leaders tended to throw overboard Christian doctrine but they wanted to keep the Christian ethic. Now we recognise that this can never be. Today the ethic has gone with the doctrine and the church has often become utterly bankrupt.

Amongst the challenges to behaviour and conduct inevitably comes the call to mission and service. One of the chapters which most poignantly galvanise Christians into action is Romans 10 with its series of questions that concern the relationship between hearing and believing. It asks us the unanswerable question 'How can they believe if they have never heard?' That chapter is towards the climax of the doctrinal section of Romans and what follows in terms of obedient service. It therefore follows that in the churches of today the best way to ensure a continuation of Christian mission and service is to be faithful in teaching the truths of Christianity. A church which is always learning will be a church ready to go out and spill over in life to others. It is vital to start at the beginning and not merely to press for commitment and service. True exposition of the word of God should lead people to begin to want to go out in service for their Lord.

The letter to the Romans could well be the crowning moment of Paul's writing. It is a summary of all that he believes about the Christian faith. No letter demonstrates more clearly the two halves of creed and conduct. In the first section of the letter Paul builds the superstructure of Christian doctrine, starting from the universality of sin and the consequent need for justification by grace through faith. The inherent sinfulness of all mankind, Jew and Gentile alike, means that all mankind needs the salvation that comes only through Jesus. It is not surprising therefore that Romans 1:16 is the clarion call of the letter. Here Paul emphasises that he is not ashamed of that gospel because it is God's power unto salvation to everyone who believes. The logic of the doctrine of justification by faith will inevitably issue in sacrificial service, for here is a message which every single person needs to hear.

There is an unusual twist in the story in Romans for after chapters 5–8, four chapters full of the wonder of the Gospel which is ours 'through Jesus Christ our Lord', comes the very controversial Romans 9–11. In these chapters Paul deals very movingly with his concern for his fellow Jews and their plan in the economy of God. Here are many issues concerning predestination and God's overruling providence. But the underlying theme is the passion of the apostle for his own people. In Romans 10:1–4 and in Romans 9:1–5 he demonstrates how much he would do if only he could reach his own people and lead them to Jesus. That heartbeat of passion every Christian needs. If we allow ourselves to think through the implications of the gospel and the barrenness of those without it we shall be able to echo the deep feeling of the apostle Paul.

Down the centuries Romans 12:1 has been a focal

point of the call of God to service. Here the apostle drives home the logic of the doctrine he has been expounding. It is a call to offer our bodies back to God as living sacrifices . Only this will match the marvellous grace of God seen in the giving of Jesus utterly and completely on the cross. But there can be no substitute sacrifice. How easy it is to imagine that the Lord would be pleased because we give him some of our time or we are generous in our gifts of money. Ultimately, though both of these matter, what the Lord wants of us is the gift of our lives in service. Nor does it speak of our souls but of our bodies, our particular functions and gifts in the service of the Lord.

This is not the call of some to special service but the call of every Christian to holiness of life and dedication to the Lord. Too often we have limited the idea of call to the special few. Within the call of every Christian to service may come a specific call to some form of Christian enterprise at home or abroad. All of this is under the umbrella of these words at the beginning of Romans 12.

There is something decisive and unique about that giving of ourselves. At Keswick many find the act of standing as an offering of the life to the Lord is such a moment. For myself it was a turning point although it took some 18 months before I recognised what was implicit in that commitment. The Lord took me at my word. I offered my life and then he told me exactly what that would mean. We must be available and then he will open the particular door which we need to enter. Because of human frailty we desperately want to see which is the door before we offer ourselves. But the Lord is more concerned about our availability than about the particular sphere of service into which we are to go.

Then alongside the dedication comes the challenge of verse 2 that we should not go on being conformed to the pattern of the world but instead be transformed. Here is the continual process and the challenge is always there. Ultimately Christian service will always be in contrast with the spirit of the world. We are not thinking about status, position or fulfilment. We are thinking only about the glory of God and the good of others. To that high calling God challenges us and offers us by the Spirit the possibility of being transformed in constant renewal.

Then the apostle reminds us that he gives different gifts and different abilities. He does not ask us to be super-gifted people. He simply asks us to use the gifts that he has given us and we shall be held responsible for these.

At the end of a letter Paul will often spend time with greetings and more personal comments. In Romans 15 he gives us an insight into his great desire to keep going outwards with the Gospel. He sees his ministry as a pioneer missionary enterprise, always on the frontier for Christ. In one sense that ministry may not be ours. But there is a challenge to Christians not to be content to build on others' foundations but always to be looking out for pastures new for the gospel. These can be interpreted geographically or racially or culturally. It may just be the constant challenge to keep reaching new people with the good news. It is all too easy to settle into a comfortable ministry for Jesus, enjoying fellowship, speaking to those who are already in sympathy with our message. Paul had a deep desire to fulfil his obligation to the grace of God to share the good news to the end of the earth while there was breath in him. May that passion never disappear from the church.

It is part of Paul's pattern of writing that he blends his testimony and the message which he has received. We need to be careful that we are not merely subjective in our teaching. On the other hand truth without the warmth of experience can be very dry and uncompelling. Read Paul's letter to the Galatians, one of his most white-hot letters, so fiery that Paul even omits the normal courtesies at the beginning of the letter. The reason behind this strong feeling is that he sees a group of people destroying the purity of the gospel by insisting on more than faith in Jesus for salvation. It is his battle with those who insist that Gentile believers should be circumcised and should conform to the Jewish legalistic fabric which makes Paul speak out so dogmatically in the letter. He reminds his readers that he had had to stand eyeball-to-eyeball with Peter and rebuke him on the same theme. Even his beloved Barnabas had been led astray because of his gentle desire not to cause upset.

But there are truths for which we must battle whatever our temperament. It is not a mark of Christian love to be tolerant of that which destroys the gospel. In every age the battle is renewed. Christian mission must ever be true to the gospel received. We may not dilute it in order to suit the spirit of the day or of a particular culture in which we minister. How to differentiate between the externals which are changeable and the essence of the gospel which is unchangeable calls for constant spiritual vigilance. But there is an unchanging Gospel, and there is an unchanging need for Christians to stand by it and to preach none other. Paul could even say in Galatians 1:8–9 that if somebody preaches any other gospel, even if he claims to be an angel from heaven, he is cursed and anathema. We may not like Paul's dogmatism but the very existence of the church depends upon it. There can be no mission which is effective unless we are true to the gospel. Once destroy that foundation and the whole rationale of mission will disappear.

One of the great battle-grounds for this truth is in the reality of our unity in Christ. Our great Keswick motto comes from this dramatic letter to the Galatians, in chapter 3 verse 28, where 'all one in Christ Jesus' is no mere slogan but a dramatic manifestation of the truth of the gospel in the breaking down of all the great barriers of that day. It no longer mattered whether you were Jew or Greek, slave or free, male or female, because your union with Christ transcended all other demarcation lines. It was possible to hold that in theory, but not to see it worked out in practice. In Paul's day that meant a battle over the problem of food laws and whether or not a Gentile believer had to be circumcised. To defend that principle Paul would indeed confront Peter and risk misunderstanding. The unity of believers in Christ must be preserved whatever the price. Not least is this important because that unity is part of the message to be preached. When Paul writes to the Ephesians he speaks in the first half of chapter 2 about the peace that we have with God through our Lord Jesus and in the second half of the chapter of the peace we have with one another through the cross of Jesus. You may not enjoy the horizontal peace without first of all discovering the vertical peace. But it would be equally incongruous to claim to have peace with God but to refuse reconciliation with our brothers. Therefore we take out to the ends of the world the truth that there is unity in Christ. Here alone can a divided, hating world find peace.

That ministry of reconciliation comes out in one of

the most stirring chapters about service in 2 Corinthians chapter 5. Here Paul is sharing with us the motivation that kept him faithful in ministry. We ought often to ask what it was that kept this man going through all the pressures and persecutions he had to endure. This chapter in 2 Corinthians gives us the secret. He reminds us that the fear of the Lord moves him to persuade men, that the love of Christ drives him on, that love which is seen in its fullness in the death of Jesus on the cross, and that the wonder of the new creation in Christ leaves him no option but to share that good news with others. For all these reasons Paul speaks of being called to be ambassadors for Christ.

This depicts a lovely blend of authority and yet insignificance. The ambassador is of no consequence in himself but he becomes important because he represents his country and his monarch. But in Paul's day the word ambassador spoke much more of the person who came from the Roman Emperor with terms of peace to a warring nation. So the Christian servant is busy with a message of reconciliation and a ministry of reconciliation. Those two should always go together. The church preaches and the church lives. The greatest evangelism is always done out of the context of a living church which demonstrates with all its imperfections the reality of a gospel of reconciliation, of peace and love.

It is significant that this great chapter about service ends with the challenge to take the message while it is still today. At the beginning of 2 Corinthians 6:1–2 Paul marvels at the privilege of being a fellow-worker with God. But that makes the urgency all the greater, for these are days of grace.

These verses come at the end of a passage which

meant much to me personally. When being called to the ordained ministry in the Church of England, I went on retreat in preparation for ordination and I was a little appalled at the prospect of hours of silence. Silence is not my normal forte nor my greatest delight. But I was encouraged to read these chapters during that period of silence because they spoke of the glory of the ministry. Somehow the Lord drove home that message and I have never forgotten the wonder that we are called as vessels of clay to take out the treasure of the gospel.

The more I realise what a great treasure the good news is, the more I recognise my own frailty and the more I marvel that the Lord can actually be glorified through our vessels of clay. Paul's argument is that because we are worth nothing the splendour of the gospel will shine even more. How careful we must be not to gild the vessels of clay and to make the personality important. In the truest sense while using our personality we are meant to hide behind the Cross so that it is the treasure which people see and not the mere vessels of clay. Nonetheless it is a great privilege and Paul has to cry in these chapters, 'Who is sufficient for these things?'

The apostle is very aware of his utter inadequacy for the task, and yet he is never slow to recite the history of his sufferings in Christian service. In 2 Corinthians 6 and 11 there is a catalogue of the things which he suffered for the sake of the gospel. Indeed he would count these as the badge of his apostleship in very marked and deliberate contrast with the marks of the super apostles whose ministry was undermining the church. For them it was a matter of the authority of their position, their intellectual status and their special visions. Paul will refuse to boast except in that which he has suffered for Christ's sake. In a moving description in 2 Corinthians 12 he contrasts the visions he has seen, of which he will not boast, with the weakness in which he will boast. Constantly we must be on our guard against a wrong concept of the marks of real spirituality. Paul would glory that he was privileged to share the fellowship of Christ's sufferings and would rejoice with his missionary friends that he was allowed to be worthy to suffer with Christ. That element needs desperately to be reinstated in a world where success is so important and where the boasting is all too often in achievements rather than in likeness to Christ.

In similar terms in his first letter to the Corinthians, Paul is at pains to condemn the personality cult and party spirit which was dividing that church. It was particularly despicable because it detracted from the message of Christ crucified which was always the heart of Paul's preaching, as it should be of ours. That message is preached as much in action as in word and constantly Paul will bring the Corinthians back to the realisation that they were 'bought with a price'.

A constant reminder of that truth will deepen our commitment and will make us very careful not just of the quality of our service but of the consistency of our lives. How often the work of a man of God has been spoiled by some tragic fall from grace and into the temptation of Satan. We do not mar the work because we ourselves are imperfect vessels. But we do bring dishonour when we trifle with sin and forget how much it cost him to redeem us. The greatest incentive for holy living is the marvel of the love of Christ seen in the self-sacrifice of Calvary. To bear the marks of Jesus means that we not only suffer with him but we crucify those things in our lives which dishonour him.

90

Themes of mission and service are integral to all Paul's writings. Some of his earliest writings are in the two letters to the Thessalonians and the theme is already well established there. Paul can rejoice that the change in the lives of these Thessalonian Christians was such a witness that he hardly needed to preach. It is hard to believe that Paul would ever keep silent, but he could honestly say that they were doing his preaching for him by the transformation in their lives. Any missionary is delighted when the Lord has so worked through his preaching that a church has been set up which is its own witness, and he can then move on to further pastures. But with the Thessalonians Paul still encourages them to holiness of life to make their continuing witness consistent, and he reminds them in a verse which has been an encouragement to so many servants of the Lord that the one who calls is faithful to do it (1 Thessalonians 5 24). Alongside that faithfulness of God is the enabling of the Spirit of God. There is always the danger that we quench his enthusiasm. Paul longed that these early Christians should never lose the thrill of that first revelation of the Spirit's power in their lives.

But the great theme of the first and second letters to the Thessalonians is that of our Lord's return. The challenge to holy living as well as to Christian service is seen in the light of those great truths, and Paul is merely echoing the constant theme of Jesus himself. This is especially true in his use of the theme of a thief in the night in 1 Thessalonians 5:4. In the light of the uncertainty of the date of our Lord's return but the certainty of the fact of it, Christians are called to be ever alert and active. 2 Thessalonians includes a very intriguing chapter about the work of anti-Christ and this reminds us that in the meantime we are not in a spiritual vacuum. Satan is very much at work and therefore we must be all the more urgent in our ministry.

There was a time when this was a high point in missionary motivation. It was the cry of Christians down the centuries to win the world in preparation for the coming of the King. Sometimes over-exaggerated emphasis on the second Advent tended to make it less credible in the eyes of thinking people. But we have turned the wheel full circle and need again to be reminded, particularly in the light of the Armageddon feeling of today, that our Lord could return at any time. We must be urgent in the light of our Lord's coming again.

It is quite erroneous to suggest that Paul lost that vision as the years went by. In the pastoral epistles Paul is still thinking of that day and looking forward to it. By now he is conscious of his own impending death and therefore spends more time encouraging Timothy and Titus in the care of the young church. But even that is in the light of the final judgement day. In a moving passage in 2 Timothy 4:1–8 the ageing apostle looks back with a clear conscience and therefore can look on with great confidence to the day when he will meet the righteous Judge. It is the mark of a man of God that he is still going on when the years have passed by. It is equally the mark of a man of God that he wants to encourage others in service. One of the joys of Christian enterprise as one gets older is seeing a younger generation taking up the mantle, no doubt with very different emphases and yet with the same message. Elisha will not be the same as Elijah but the same Spirit is at work. Sad the person who cannot believe that in God's economy the best is yet to be.

The letters to Ephesus and Colossae are often seen as very much church letters and Paul sees the whole church as a missionary enterprise. It is through the unity and life of the church that the Gospel is seen. Missionary service at every level is not just that of individual pioneers thrusting forward but of a whole church community radiating the light of Christ in every dark place. Watchman Nee's little book on Ephesians sums up the thrust of that letter: 'Sit, walk, stand'. The letter is very much divided into those three commands. We are meant to enjoy the riches of the gospel, to live consistently by it, and then to expect a fight on our hands. It is as the church is sitting and enjoying Christ that others are attracted. It is even more as Christians walk consistently that they make Jesus real. And at all times there will be a battle when the church begins to live at this level. We shall continue to wrestle against satanic forces till the final age.

There is a consistency in the New Testament letters on this theme of mission and service. The Apostle John may use very different language from that of Paul but he picks up this theme of the witness of the church and in his letters points out that it is by walking in light and walking in love that the church commends the Gospel and the Saviour. In a very practical letter John insists that we cannot claim to be children of God unless we show love and unless there is the light of moral living. No service will be effective if we deny the truth of the Gospel by the way we live. John reminds us that God is light and God is love. These are not merely dogmas to be proclaimed but truths to be exhibited.

Peter's first letter is full of reminiscences of his relationship with Jesus, and the careful student can find there many echoes of the Gospels. Perhaps strangely the note is not so much of Peter the fisherman reaching out after his commission to become a fisher of men, as Peter the pastor learning to be a good shepherd. Of course the letters went to Christian fellowships and Peter's pastoral heart comes out very much in his letter. But he does see the church as being the community which must proclaim the deeds of Christ. Using good Old Testament analogies 1 Peter 2:9 sees the church as the new Israel and the task of the new church is to 'declare the wonderful deeds of him who called you out of darkness into his marvellous light'. Indeed the quotation begins with a picture of what the church is, 'a chosen race, a royal priesthood, a holy nation, God's own people' so that it may declare God's deeds.

In some ways this again brings echoes of our Lord's words to Peter. Right at the very beginning of Peter's call Jesus recognised in Simon one who could become Peter, the Rock man. The process by which the unstable Simon became the rocklike Peter was long and tortuous. But the Lord saw the potential in Peter. Once he became what the Lord meant him to be, he would be a great agent of the gospel. That has lasting truth. It is a great encouragement to all of us that the Lord saw potential in us, and still does in spite of our imperfections and our slowness to respond. Equally we must ever see the potential in others and the possibility of the Lord using their gifts to take the gospel on a stage further in its march throughout the world.

In this synopsis of the letters of the New Testament we may note that 2 Peter and Jude are full of the danger of false apostles and false teaching. The church always needs to be on the alert. We see from Scripture and from church history that the devil loves to infiltrate into the life of the church. How often an enterprising missionary project has been ruined because false teaching has come in and personalities not in tune with God have wrecked what started in such a promising way. We must always be on the alert because Satan never wearies.

The epistle to the Hebrews with its anonymous authorship majors on the wonder of the finished work of Christ and the reality of his High Priesthood. In a sense it is the absence of the risen Lord that lies behind our commission to go into all the world, and indeed to follow the example of Jesus and to dare to go to him outside the camp (Hebrews 13:13). If the reality of what Christ did on the cross is the motivation for service, equally the presence of the risen Lord who is the same yesterday, today and for ever (Hebrews 13:8) is our inspiration.

Inspiration is also found in chapter 11 of this great letter in looking back at the great heroes of faith. These are the great cloud of witnesses that surround us challenging and encouraging us. If Abraham and Moses and other great Old Testament heroes could risk in faith, how much more we who have the finality of the truth in Jesus. They could endure all kinds of hardship because they saw the invisible God. They could set out on impossible journeys because they believed God had called them. It would be tragic if the Christian church was outshone by the active faith of these Old Testament saints. So Hebrews 12:1–2 challenges us to go out not only following their example but looking away to Jesus who will ever be the most perfect illustration of faith and sacrifice.

The Book of the Revelation as a climax to Scripture should be the final impetus to faithfulness in service. Sadly it has all too often been the battleground of theories, all of which claim to be absolutely true to Scripture and yet often miss out the ultimate challenge of the book. These words of the apostle John in exile were not written as an enigma or a riddle. They were written to encourage Christians to be steadfast in the hour of testing. However you interpret the details of that glorious book it speaks of the victory of Jesus now, beginning with a vision of the risen, ascended, glorified Christ, and the assurance that the Lamb upon the throne is sovereign. There is a panoramic view of the victory of Christ both present and future. All this was meant to stimulate Christians in the hour of persecution to remain loyal. Here is the unveiling which gave John and his readers an insight into what is happening beyond our normal sight. When it looks as if the church is down and out, as if Satan is triumphing we need to recollect that the Lord is on the throne and that his return and final reign are sure.

In the light of that the letters to the seven churches at the beginning of Revelation have a message to every age. It is not only individuals who should be challenged to service but whole churches. It would be foolish to try to see some strange survey of church history in these letters. But each one of them deserves study.

Sometimes the Lord comes to us to remind us that we have lost our first love, as with the church in Ephesus. Sometimes he has to remind us that churches which have a name for being alive have really died as with Sardis. Sometimes he needs to encourage us like the small church at Philadelphia with a great open door to reach out with the good news. Sometimes he comes as to the church at Laodicea with a solemn warning of the dangers of complacency. Yet the great encouragement is that though Jesus spoke to this church some of the most appalling words that ever fell from his lips, he also gave it one of the most glorious invitations. He told them that their lukewarmness made him sick. But he also told them that he was standing at the door knocking and waiting to take over.

Maybe those words of warning come to us. How can we be lukewarm about the Gospel of such a great Saviour? But it does happen. Perhaps we need to hear afresh the voice of the risen Lord Jesus who goes on knocking, and we need to open the door to him so that we might go through the open door that he has for us.

7: I Was There

Scripture not only contains the call to mission and service, it becomes the vehicle through which the Spirit goes on doing his work. Every preacher and teacher will know the unique and yet humbling thrill of being an instrument whereby God works today through his Word interpreted by his servant. It ought to be as true today as in Scripture itself that whenever men and women of God proclaim the Word of God they should expect the Spirit of God to be at work in some signal way. I believe that we see so little because we expect so little. There is no miracle like the miracle of the Word of God becoming alive today with power to transform lives in every way, not least in this great theme of mission and service.

For many people the Keswick Convention has been the place of confrontation and this book is within that particular context. But of course that is only one of the major arenas where this happens. Indeed if in every church and meeting place the Word of God was preached with the same confidence in the Spirit of God, perhaps Keswick Conventions and the like would cease to have their place and importance. What matters is the confrontation between the living Word of God and the person in the contemporary world waiting to discover God's will and purpose. That combination has dynamic possibilities.

Two people, almost chosen at random, speak of what Keswick meant to them in the awareness of God's call. Roger Kennedy, now with the Scripture Gift Mission, hails from West Cumberland and spent much of his childhood in Keswick. It is good to be able to record that not only do visitors from the whole world find inspiration at the Keswick Convention but it has its power in the immediate locality. Roger can remember listening when he was only three or four to a famous speaker of a bygone age, Guy King, and he recollects the days of the duck boards and much water in and around the tent. Within his experience of more than fifty years' contact with the Convention he has a particular awareness of God at work in his life at a time when he was thinking seriously about his Christian service.

But it is significant that the first impact of the Convention was not in a call to Christian work but in being made aware of the reality of sin and the demand to put things right immediately. In this ministry Keswick has had a significant role in many people's lives. For Roger Kennedy it was the young people's meetings to which he cycled in those early days that brought home this particular challenge. Year by year he was brought under the conviction of the Word of God about a life made clean by the Spirit of God. A call to service must always be earthed in that challenge to holiness without which service is pointless and hypocritical.

Roger Kennedy lived with an atmosphere of missionary service in his own home where missionaries often visited, but it was at Keswick that he made his open commitment as he stood at the missionary meeting indicating a readiness to serve if

God called. In those days commitments were not registered, but in Roger's heart and mind a stand had been made. Two years later in the Army the clear call came to go as a missionary to India. For 17 years Roger worked in Christian publishing work in that great land, and so the ministry of Keswick had its repercussions thousands of miles away from the place where the call came.

Roger's ministry in India continued to have links with Keswick. He recollects coming back on his first furlough and being refused admittance to the young people's meetings where there was strict control in those days. Apparently he was still within the age bracket but missionary service had taken its toll of his appearance! But those furloughs in Keswick were not the sum total of the influence of the Convention on his service. His experience in Keswick of the unity of believers in Christ prepared him for ministry in India in a completely interdenominational fellowship. It is easy to take for granted the wonder of that reality of 'all one in Christ Jesus'. It is too precious to lose and that influence of Keswick has shaped many manifestations of Christian service throughout the world transcending denominational and secondary considerations. For some time Roger served on the Committee of the Evangelical Fellowship of India which would often invite Keswick speakers to minister in that country as part of the worldwide influence of the Convention movement. This still happens and it would be impossible to find time to record how many countries have been enriched through the ministry which started at Keswick.

My most recent personal experience of the ministry of the Keswick Convention overseas was a visit to the lovely island of Barbados where most of the other visitors were sunning themselves endlessly on the seashore. I was caught up with a week's Bible teaching ministry quite openly called the Barbados Keswick. In an island with much deep religion and inevitably many religious undercurrents and debates, there was something very refreshing about the united testimony of 'all one in Christ Jesus'. It was intriguing and yet a great privilege to explain to interviewers on radio and television the relationship between what happened in a lakeland town a century ago and what was happening in the baking heat of Barbados in 1988. In every way these two places were a thousand miles apart. But there was a continuum of the message and a great sense of the same spirit and inspiration.

It was equally fascinating to minister alongside a young Jamaican colleague who had never been to Keswick in England and yet clearly preached the message from Keswick with its emphasis on biblical exposition, a call to holiness of life, and a challenge to service. It was yet another testimony to the world wide influence of the ministry from Keswick and also a reminder of its contemporary relevance and power.

Roger comments that of course missionary service is changing. The call to service while in one sense eternal, is different in the world of today with so many countries having their own Christian leadership and needing less support from expatriate missionaries. Nonetheless he strongly hopes that Keswick will never lose its world vision and its challenge in motivation for mission in the world. It is still a thrill in his ministry in the Scripture Gift Mission to meet overseas visitors coming to Keswick for the Convention and to see how the ministry of Keswick continues in that way. It may be that our primary ministry now is not to export missionaries, although that will continue, but to encourage national Christians to be more effective in their ministry and true to the message which has inspired the Keswick Convention down the years.

Moira McInnes heard her call to missionary service at a much later Keswick, in 1981. Moira became a Christian through an epilogue at her church youth club, which must be an encouragement to all faithful and often frustrated youth leaders. She trained as a nursery nurse and was working in that capacity when she became aware of the Lord saying something to her about service overseas. This began in her home church, a reminder of the relationship between the local church and the wider ministry of Conventions. The challenge was from Ephesians 2:10, which reminds us that although we are saved by grace through faith we are created in Christ Jesus to do good works. The very wonder of our forgiveness challenges us to share with others. With that in the background of her mind Moira came to Keswick in 1981.

She suggests in her testimony that her commitment to full-time service at the Convention was somewhat reluctant. Often the servants of God respond without all the enthusiasm that God might desire. Even though reluctant and half-hearted, Peter could be used to bring in a shoal of fish in the lake of Galilee when he obeyed. Many of us have found God's blessing even when we have responded somewhat reluctantly. But the challenge came through the missionary service and the message in Jeremiah chapter 18 about the potter and the clay. It was a reminder to Moira that God had sovereignty over her life and that she had to respond to the gentle but firm working of his hand on her life to be the kind of vessel he could use in service. Paul would use the analogy of being a vessel of clay, and at best we are always weak so that the honour is his not ours. God is not concerned about how wonderful the vessel is but only for the glory of his name through his servant. That should be our greatest ambition as it became Moira's.

Moira's call to service at Keswick was not her first nor her last visit to the Convention. She testifies to the joy of being part of a great crowd at the Convention, the singing and the fellowship, but most of all the Word of God which kept on working in her life until there came the yielding of obedience. From that moment in 1981 Moira went on to train for service and was accepted by the Africa Inland Mission to work in Tanzania, where she went in 1985. Her great desire is to be back in Keswick on her first furlough for refreshment and renewal.

Looking back on her call to service through that challenge of Jeremiah Moira counts it a privilege that she, apparently so insignificant, could still be personally addressed by the great God in a great Convention. For that reason Keswick is very special to her and she has met so many others who similarly have found the Convention to be not only a meeting place with God but a sending out place from God. There is nothing special about Keswick. This book only uses the Keswick Convention as an illustration of what God is doing and can be doing. But it does hammer home the message that in the context of the exposition of the truth of God's Word and its personal call to holiness there can be a powerful and irresistible call to go out with the same message to a world in the same kind of need.

Not only does the Lord call individuals to service through the ministry of the Keswick Convention, it is also significant that down the years many missionary societies have had close links with Keswick and many see the Convention as their birth place. In an age when inevitably, with changing circumstances in the world Christian scene, there are fewer missionary societies being born, it is good for us to stop and recollect what God has done in this way and how much world mission owes to the ministry at Keswick. Some of these facts are recorded not with any sense of pride in a movement. In Keswick as in every other aspect of Christian work there is much of which we are not proud. But it is right to give thanks to God for ways in which he has used a Convention for the deepening of spiritual life to promote the spread of the Gospel throughout the world. The burden of this book is to point out that those two things must ever go together however much the scene may change.

Many evangelical societies have links with Keswick in one way or another and it would be impossible to be exhaustive in our comments about the relationship. But there are some very significant landmarks. For example the Africa Evangelical Fellowship sprang from the South African General Mission which had its birth at Keswick. Spencer Walton, who was born in 1850, committed himself to a preaching ministry in 1882 and at the Keswick Convention met Andrew Murray, who was already involved in evangelism through the Dutch Reformed Church in South Africa. Andrew Murray had come to Europe for a cure for his strained voice and from that unusual beginning this missionary society found its birth. Andrew Murray encouraged Spencer Walton at Keswick to go to South Africa. Eventually in 1889 they formed the Cape General Mission which in due course became the South Africa General Mission. Spencer Walton's wife had been brought to Christ at the Keswick Convention and therefore not surprisingly Walton and Murray started an annual Convention which became known as the South African Keswick.

In 1903 the Japan Evangelistic Band came to birth at Keswick. Paget Wilkes and Barclay Buxton, who were already ministering in Japan, were at the Keswick Convention while home on furlough. At the vicarage of the parish church at Keswick a special meeting was called to consider forming a band of missionaries to go to Japan. The vicar's wife, Mrs Herbert Wood, was convinced that this was God's will at a half-night of prayer held in the vicarage after the Convention meeting. The very next day she encountered a Miss Estelle Edmeads who was interested in the work in Japan and in God's perfect timing by the evening her passage money and support had been pledged. In October of that year she left for Japan and Paget Wilkes went back to Kobe which became the centre of the work of the Japan Evangelistic Band. There are still many echoes of Keswick in the evangelical ministry in that city and elsewhere in Japan. Those of us who have been privileged to minister in Japan know how deep these roots go, and although we cannot live in the past we rejoice that this is the heritage which has enriched the witness to Christ in a country where the church is numerically so small. Great things grow from little births.

The year 1911 saw the birth of a Keswick link with South America in the formation of the Evangelical Union of South America. The Edinburgh Conference of the previous year had not considered South America as a mission field because of the Roman Catholic influence there. This was brought to the attention of the Keswick Convention and as a result EUSA came into being, largely through the influence of Stuart Holden of the Keswick Convention Council.

One of the most memorable missionary links with Keswick is through Amy Carmichael whose writings have been an inspiration to so many people down the years. The Dohnavur Fellowship formed in 1926 really began through Amy Carmichael's work at Dohnavur starting in 1901. Amy had a very significant relationship with Robert Wilson, one of the co-founders of the Keswick Convention. She had heard him speak in Glasgow and Belfast and he became a firm friend of the family, affectionately known by Amy as 'the DOM' (dear old man). At Robert Wilson's invitation Amy went to the Keswick Convention in 1888 and wrote, 'It was an unforgettable time; it meant a new committal of one's whole life.' She lived as a daughter with Robert Wilson while he was Chairman of the Convention and heard the call to missionary service in 1892 with China very much in mind. During her time at the Convention that year she dedicated herself for missionary service in that great land.

Robert Wilson's predecessor as Chairman had not allowed the tent to be used for missionary meetings in spite of pleas from Hudson Taylor. Unofficially it was lent in 1886 and 1887 and some 30 young people offered for missionary service in that latter year. In the missionary meeting of 1888 £10 was sent to the Chairman as the nucleus of a fund for sending out Keswick missionaries and Amy Carmichael was the first to be supported in this way. It is strange to reflect that missionary endeavour was not there at the very beginning but was a very early offshoot of the work of the Spirit in the Convention.

Amy Carmichael's missionary service had a chequered beginning. The China Inland Mission turned down Amy's offer for health reasons and her brief period in Japan ended with ill health. But in 1895 Amy was accepted for work at Bangalore, once more at a meeting in Keswick. She arrived in India in November of that year and remained there until her death in January 1951. In 1901 she began her children's work when a seven-year-old girl came to her after escaping from a Hindu temple. She worked to provide a home and Christian upbringing for children in South India and formed the Dohnavur Fellowship in 1926. Once more the Lord used the challenge of the Keswick Convention to initiate pioneer missionary endeavour. In Amy Carmichael's case it went further and because of her own deep spirituality very much based on her Keswick experience Amy was able to write poetry which has gripped the hearts of many searching Christians to this day.

Indirectly there have been many other missionary links with Keswick. Chairmen of the Keswick Convention Council in the past have included directors of the Overseas Missionary Fellowship (formerly the China Inland Mission) and the Bible Churchman's Missionary Society. We are delighted that these links remain on the present Council. There is also a fascinating story in the links between Keswick and the Buxton family, who were used of the Lord in missionary service in Japan and Africa as well as helping to found the Inter-Varsity Fellowship and work amongst students in this country. All Nations Bible College also had its origins in the Buxton family and indeed is based at the former home of that family. The grace of God has so worked that especially in the early days of this century the Keswick Convention formed an important and influential meeting ground and springboard for world mission.

Rejoicing at this history we are mindful that, living

in a very different world context, there must ever be a relationship between the challenge to holiness at Keswick and the life of service. Emphasis on holiness without service can lead to unhealthy introspection. The challenge to service without a deep foundation in a life of holiness can be superficial activism. It may well be that, like many missionary societies, Keswick needs constantly to have a fresh look at the manner in which this challenge is brought. But it is the intention of the present Keswick Council that the relationship between the teaching ministry of the Convention and the call to service will continue and by God's grace we shall see yet another chapter being written in this imposing history.

8: Mission 2000

Repetition has good precedent in Christian teaching. The apostle Paul was a master at getting across the same message in different ways because he knew that it needed to be driven home remorselessly. So this book is trying to get across the message that mission and service always follow from true spiritual renewal. The ministry of the Keswick Convention has concentrated on holiness of life, but inevitably almost from the beginning that led to a great upsurge in missionary zeal and an emphasis on service in the world. Historically as well as biblically this has always been true. It is therefore wise for the Christian church prayerfully and in ministry to concentrate on the need for personal and corporate renewal in the Spirit through the teaching and preaching of the Word of God. We need not fear when exposition is faithfully done that there will be unhealthy introspection. The Word of God is always sending renewed people out into the world. It is a mark of a person who has known the Spirit in his or her life, that there is a great desire to share with others. Thus it was that Jesus in his famous last words in Acts 1:8 promised the disciples that they would experience the power of the Spirit coming upon them. Then they would be witnesses in a ministry that would take them to the ends of the earth. But before

111

ever they could go out in service they had to wait in Jerusalem for the promise of the Father.

Today we urgently need to be renewed in our trust and confidence in the Word of God as well as in the power of the Spirit of God. Evangelism will only be a priority when evangelicalism is in its rightful place.

Sometimes these two words are confused. I am often invited to speak at a gathering which I am told will be 'evangelical'. Long ago I discovered that this word always meant 'evangelistic'. I sometimes gently remind people that I cannot preach anything other than an evangelical message, but I am very happy to concentrate on an evangelistic message when that is the order of the day. Ultimately evangelism, which means sharing the good news, will only stem from evangelicalism, which means preserving and holding on to the good news. There is a kind of evangelism which is fearful of evangelicalism. There are those who want to share but are very unsure about what to share. It is possible for there to be an arid evangelicalism which holds on to the truth but seems sadly lacking in a desire to share it. The clarion call at this point in time is for the church of today to rejoice in the deposit of truth given to us in the New Testament and in seeing its wonder to go out with it urgently to a hungry world.

I am writing these words at the beginning of the year 1988. Years ago I studied history at Oxford University and learned that historical movements are always far more complex than had first been imagined. Sometimes I cynically began to think that even if things had been simple the historian would have to make them more complex in order to demonstrate erudition. But it is a fact and even the great movements of Reformation were not always

112

gloriously spiritual. On the other hand there is no doubt that the Spirit of God was at work in that glorious Reformation and the year 1988 has two very significant anniversaries of that time.

In the year 1588 the Spanish Armada was driven away from our shores, largely by a change of wind. The straightforward English believers of those days could coin the Latin phrase 'Deus afflavit et dissipati sunt' – 'God blew and they were destroyed'. Was it as simple as all that? It is hard to be dogmatic but we do rejoice that the nation could well have been saved from the dominance yet again of a dead religion.

In the year 1688 came the Glorious Revolution when William of Orange became King of England. Once more history records that he landed in this country with his entourage because of a very favourable 'protestant wind'. Whatever the power behind the elements, there is no doubt that once more our country was preserved for a reformed religion and these issues are still important.

It is good to be able to rejoice today that many of the barriers between Protestantism and Roman Catholicism are being broken. It is even more a cause for joy that many Roman Catholics are discovering new life in the Word of God and the Spirit of God, and it is equally important to remember that much of Protestantism has become dead and liberal. There are situations when an evangelical Anglican often has more in common with a born-again Roman Catholic than he does with some of his unbelieving brethren in his own denomination. Nonetheless the great truths of the Reformation, not least the authority of Scripture and the sufficiency of the work of Christ, must be preserved and in 1988 we do well to celebrate these two significant anniversaries.

1988 also sees the anniversary of the conversion of John Wesley 250 years ago. There have been few greater milestones in church history in Britain. With his brother Charles, under God John revolutionised church life in this country. Even secular historians have commented that the movement which began through their preaching helped to save this country from the equivalent of the French Revolution. It was a different kind of revolution and much of this was stimulated by marvellous hymnology, particularly that of Charles. Even today some of the great hymns of Charles Wesley are used by the Spirit to lead people into an abiding relationship with Jesus. Hymns like 'And can it be', 'Jesus lover of my soul', 'Hark the herald angels sing' are full of deep theology which blend the truths of the past with the experience of the present. In a marvellously poetic way they pick up the great themes of the New Testament and enrich not only our worship but our spirituality as we ponder the words. It is a great joy that hymns are being written again today and some of them are memorable, but it is doubtful whether many will survive as have these masterpieces from Charles Wesley. In that remarkable way the moving of God's Spirit in the lives of these men of God a quarter of a millenium ago is still bearing fruit still today, enriching the lives of God's people, deepening their understanding of God's Word and sending them out in obedient service.

It is a commonplace that the experience of John Wesley in the meeting house in London was based upon a reading from Luther's commentary on the Epistle to the Romans. Although John Wesley may never have used the word 'conversion' of that experience, there is no doubt about its revolutionary nature. To ponder the men whose lives were transformed by the letter to the Romans is to remind ourselves afresh of the power of that living Word. Augustine, Martin Luther, John Wesley, were all mighty men of the Spirit and all of them found new life when confronted by the Word of God written to the Christians at Rome. Then ponder the effect of these men on the history of the church, and we bow in adoration at the dynamic of the truth of God when let loose amongst the people of God.

With his new life John Wesley travelled the highways and byways of the country relentlessly. His new life and new vision drove him on and through his faithful ministry thousands of lives were transformed. Once more we are back to the old truth that a spiritual experience should always lead to an outgoing ministry. The Church of England was largely unable to take it, and not always has Methodism continued it, but the challenge of John Wesley remains.

There have been many spurious movements since those days, as well as a continuing work of the Spirit. It is a mark of a spurious movement that it sends Christians inward and develops a ghetto mentality. Often it seems to be biblically based and yet how can it be of the Spirit when it does not drive Christians out into the world? There is a false pietism which develops an obsession with fellowship and mutual care to the exclusion of concern for a dying world. Ultimately the two should go together and indeed it is the love and care of Christians which is the springboard for effective evangelism, as well as a witness to it. But we need to be careful that we do not allow Satan to twist the genuine message of the New Testament into a perversion which unhealthily turns us in on ourselves rather than out into the world for which Christ died.   There has also been a false movement away from the basic truths of the New Testament into an ecumenism which extols unity at the cost of everything else. Another anniversary of the moment is that in celebration of the famous Edinburgh Conference which was a great milestone in the history of the ecumenical movement. But since those days very often ecumenism and evangelism have been seen as opposites rather than inextricably linked together. When Jesus in John 17 prayed that famous prayer in which he longed for the unity of the body of Christ, he also prayed about truth and love. Always these must go together and there can never be any unity apart from the truth of the Gospel. Once we have lost our moorings in the Word of God, a false ecumenism will arise. One of the great joys of the Keswick Convention movement is that it rejoices in a unity in Christ which transcends denomination and indeed makes denominational barriers seem pointless. But the point of unity is an agreement on the truth of God's Word and its relevance for every age.

A true biblical renewal will save us from false pietism and false ecumenism. It will send Christians out both in social concern and with evangelistic zeal. There should be no polarisation since both are there in the scriptural challenges in the Old and New Testaments. The prophets thundered their message of God's concern more for justice than for religious practices. Jesus in Matthew 25 had some very disturbing things to say about those who talked about their faith but neglected to show love and care to the least of his brethren. On the other hand there are those who have so diluted the Christian message that it becomes nothing more than a concern for the social well-being of men and women throughout the world. Man does not live by bread alone, ever, and no Christian can be content with mere social amelioration.

How tragic that somehow we have allowed this polarisation. Mercifully evangelicals in our day have rediscovered their heritage in social activity and sometimes the pendulum has swung too far in the other direction. A movement like the Keswick Convention is not unmindful of the social context in which holiness must be lived. But it will constantly remind us from God's Word that millions are dying without Christ and ultimately that is a fate worse than dying of starvation. James does not tell us that we should not preach to the hungry. He only reminds us that we cannot preach without feeding him first.

There is a great roll call of evangelicals who have been in the forefront of social care and reform. Names like William Wilberforce, the Earl of Shaftesbury, Dr Barnardo, William Booth of the Salvation Army – all of these and many more have demonstrated that the Gospel of salvation through faith in Christ is a stimulus to a sacrificial care for the bodies as well as the souls of needy people. In our day TEAR Fund has been a signal illustration of this same dynamic balance. All are being true to our Lord's great commission which always goes alongside the great commandment to love our neighbour as well as to love the Lord. Or again there is the balance of salt and light – the gentle pervasive influence going on all the time like salt, and the open, clear witness like light. We are told to go out and make disciples and we are told to go out and let the light of our good works shine.

We live in a rapidly changing world and sometimes as Christians we find it hard to acknowledge just how revolutionary that change has been. It is still easy to think of the Third World as being those nations who are recipients of our charity. Christian love should never be patronising. It is never one-way traffic. In these days the Third World is giving as well as receiving. There are great stories of missionary endeavour from countries which very recently were missionary-receiving nations. On a recent visit to Korea I was thrilled to learn about missionaries being sent out from that remarkable country into many parts of the world. I had a very unusual experience some years ago when I commissioned some missionaries going out from the plateau area of north Nigeria to serve in the district around Lake Chad, and then flew on ahead and was present at Lake Chad to receive them in their missionary area. Not many preachers have both commissioned and received missionaries in this kind of way. But it was a very moving experience, for here were people moving away from their own culture just as surely as people from the Western world going out to Africa and settling into a very alien environment for the sake of the Gospel.

In this context there is an urgent call which needs to be sounded loud and clear. Many people feel that the pioneer missionary spirit is not needed today, yet perhaps it was never more needed. The Christian world map has changed and the resurgence of lively churches in many parts of the world has revolutionised missionary service. But in some ways this different world scene demands even more in terms of sacrificial service. It may be that a whole lifetime's commitment to one particular area of the world will be less and less the sacrifice demanded. Sometimes it will call for flexibility and a willingness for short-term service. The Lord demands complete allegiance and a willingness to go anywhere and do anything for him. But he does not necessarily ask us to give all our life to a particular job or any particular country, although that will still be the call for some and must not be forgotten.

I want to suggest several ways in which the challenge of today, with its uniqueness, calls for that spirit of wholehearted dedication which should be the badge of the true Christian disciple. When Paul asks us in Romans 12:1 in the light of the wonder of the Gospel to give our bodies a living sacrifice, it is a call for every age, and in these latter years of the 20th century if the Lord delays his return until that magical year 2000 it has special urgent connotations.

In the first place mission 2000 will be worked out in the context of resurgent religions. Islam in particular with its militancy will continue and we need to match fundamentalism with fundamentalism, yet with a difference. Tragically a renewed Islam is often matched by an anaemic and apologetic Christianity. There is nothing in the militant spirit of fundamentalist Islam which we need to capture but it is possible to have a fundamental belief in the truths of Scripture and the uniqueness of Jesus and yet convey this belief with love and grace. We need not apologise to wish to lead Moslems to faith in Jesus but we certainly cannot hope to achieve it without loving understanding and positive dialogue. You can be dogmatic and still wear a smile.

The challenge of this renewed Islam is not only in the Middle East but on our doorstep. The possibility of mission in Britain is now greater than ever and we need to capture the vision of reaping a harvest here. It will call for the whole church working together. Often the immigrant population is to be found where the traditional churches are at their weakest and therefore there must be concerted, united, prayerful action on the part of the church as a whole. Islam may dominate the scene but other religions too have become more self-confident. Mission 2000 therefore is not ministering in a vacuum but in the midst of much religious activity.

Mission 2000 is also in the context of a sense of Armageddon in the air. The doomsters are not now the rather more extreme Christians who seem to delight in pronouncing the hour of judgement. Indeed the old hell-fire preaching has almost disappeared and we could perhaps do with its return in a 20th century garb. But doom is being pronounced, often by politicians and scientists who fear that the end cannot be far away unless attitudes change radically. It is not unchristian to want to cash in on a situation which is alive with possibilities. For we know what the end is and we know the message both of heaven and of hell. We do not know the time but we can read the signs of the times, and therefore the world should be ready to hear what Christians have to say. Where others have a sense of panic, we have a message of hope. Our Lord did tell us in such a day to lift up our heads for our redemption draws near. He also told us not to miss the opportunity but to redeem the time. It is more than tragic that when urgency is in the air in the world, the church has often lost its confidence in the apocalyptic message of the last days.

Not least mission 2000 will be earthed in a church which is ambivalent about moral standards. So often Christians are perplexed by what they see around them, even within the life of the church. In some ways this is the result of the Spirit at work in frontier situations. As in the Acts of the Apostles we are seeing people come to Christ without any background of biblical standards at all and there is therefore the urgent need to teach what the Bible demands in terms of holy living with regard to the use of our body, our time, our money and our attitudes to the world around us. Years ago Christian doctrine was diluted or even thrown overboard altogether, and yet a nation wanted to keep Christian ethics. We have, to our peril, discovered that the one cannot exist without the other. Many who lament the decline of Christian moral standards have lived for years with a healthy agnosticism towards Christian doctrine. A generation has arisen which has shown an equally cavalier attitude to Christian ethics, and there was a kind of logic about that response. But there are signs of a turning of the tide. The world is awaiting a positive Christian morality to go alongside a positive Christian message. We can only proclaim the doctrine if we live out morally the message.

We are living through days when there have been revelations from the United States of moral scandal and battles in the Church of England to uphold clear biblical standards of sexuality. Unless Christians deal honestly and courageously with these moral issues our voice will not be heard. There cannot be an effective missionary zeal from a church which has compromised its moral standards without repentance. With the awful spectre of AIDS stalking the world we are in a position to demonstrate that the standards of the Bible not only make sense and are ultimately attractive, they are the only way in which the fabric of our world will be kept intact. The Maker's instructions must be obeyed if the Maker's world is to be kept on course. Therefore mission 2000 will stem from a renewed and purified church. It could well be a traumatic time of suffering and pain within the church, but the Bible insists that life comes from that kind of death to self.

Mission 2000 must have cosmic proportions. With the media making the world shrink daily we cannot avoid the sufferings of the whole of creation. It is possible to look back over just a few months of life and tot up the disasters that have moved and challenged us. In the light of all these it is easy to seek an escape, either by a comfortable belief in the sovereignty of God which leaves us unscathed, or by spontaneous, sporadic charitable gifts or acts. But neither of these leaves any mark on our world. We may of course be so upset by all that we see that we lose faith in a caring, loving God. Or we may see this travail of creation as promised in Scripture, as an overwhelming challenge to prayerful, consistent action both in social concern and in spreading the gospel while yet there is time. What we may not do is hide ourselves away in some comfortable, parochial, self-indulgent Christian party. The stakes are too high and the hour is too late.

Nor may we in mission 2000 leave Satan out of account. In some way we have become obsessed by Satan and sometimes that is one of his more subtle weapons. It is true that he works through the occult and it is tragically true that there are satanists who have their own sinister religion and times of prayer and fasting. But I believe it would be idle to imagine that this is Satan's greatest weapon as we approach 2000. It is important in the first place to recollect that Satan is only allowed by the sovereignty of God. Nor would we be wise to assume that we know what hour we have reached in the story of Satan. Nor should we be in any sense terrified by his activity since we have the victory in Christ. But the greatest danger is that we might not see what he is doing. Paul suggests that we should not be ignorant of his devices. All too often we are.

Satan delights to steer Christians away from the truth of Scripture. He loves vague and woolly believers who live by experience and drive spiritually by the seat of their pants. He fears when he sees Christians with the Word of God open and on their knees in prayerful response. He is clearly also in his satanic wisdom having a go at the moral purity of Christians, especially those in leadership. Therefore we need to be on our guard and to be in prayer for ourselves and for one another. Satan delights to make the gospel seem unattractive because the lives of Christians are inconsistent. Not least Satan always wants to keep us away from evangelistic enterprise. Cosy introspective Christians are his pets. They cause him no trouble and never take the attack into his domain. It was C T Studd, the great fiery missionary who loved to run a rescue shop within a yard of hell. That is the spirit we need afresh, remembering Jesus' promise that in this battle with evil 'the gates of hell will not prevail'.

Yet mission 2000 is also in the context of unique opportunities to reach the whole world for Christ through modern media and particularly through the advent of the satellite. There are problems about this kind of instant communication. Yet surely the Lord has given us this marvellous means of projecting the good news into the whole world for a purpose. Tragically if those who believe in the Gospel do not buy up the opportunity either the powers of evil will or the weird manifestations of Christianity which are more likely to lead astray than to lead to Christ.

Perhaps one of the most urgent subjects for prayer is the release of Christian money on an unprecedented scale to make this ministry possible, and with it people with maturity and zeal to see that it is used aright. This will never be a substitute for the age-old one-to-one ministry and the work of the local church which must always be paramount. Thereby hangs a tale, for the present scale of Christian giving hardly allows us to continue the kind of ministry we are now doing, let alone project into this space-age mentality. But the Lord is saying something to us. This a vision for mission 2000 will certainly not leave me and I hope it may, even through these pages perhaps, stir some to a commitment which will be costly, yet which is urgently necessary.

The year 2000 will probably see city life become even more significant. The shrinking world is nowhere more obvious than in the dull reproduction of city life throughout the world. We may lament this movement and despair at the problems it will bring. But here is the centre for Christian witness and mission for years to come. Even in New Testament days the apostle Paul strategically went from city to city primarily in his ministry. Every individual counts and every soul matters to God. But the city is where the people are in their millions and where all too often sin rides triumphant. The strategy for mission 2000 must be to keep cities in the forefront of our thinking and our action. Because city life will become so similar the world over, it actually solves many problems of culture orientation. Somehow there could be a city strategy with world significance.

But we must not be too fascinated by the year 2000. If Satan loves to keep our vision low, he also sometimes delights in making Christians so busy planning for the future that they may miss the opportunity of the present. And the year 2000 may actually never reach us. Certainly there will be people reading these words for whom 2000 will never come. Therefore there is an unchanging challenge in the contemporary gospel. Now is always the day of salvation.

Equally we must beware of the temptation to imagine that massive problems in the world demand a radical reappraisal of the gospel. We do need to make the unchanging Gospel relevant to a changing world and we must not allow the conservatism in most of us to draw us back from revolutionary changes in our manner of presentation where that is necessary. But there must be no panic and certainly no compromise. Only the unchanging gospel of Jesus for the unchanging needs of people in the changing world will do.

In a sense, paradoxically perhaps, the urgency of the hour is driving us back through a lot of woolly liberalism to the basics of the New Testament Gospel. For a world which has lost direction and foundations there can be no substitute for the unerring and unique Word of God in the Gospel.

9: In and Out

The cynic in me sometimes believes that balanced Christianity is despised these days. It seems that only in the extreme is excitement to be found.

Yet Scripture is always asking for balance, which is never compromise but holding on to the truths of Scripture which sometimes seem to be at opposite ends of the spectrum. For example the Christian who takes Scripture seriously must believe in God's sovereignty and pre-destinating power, and yet at the same time believe that he wants all men to be saved and that we have the freedom to choose or reject.

When many movements abound in the religious world it is vital for Christians to be discerning and to have a balanced biblical judgement. One of the balances we need is in the realm of change. There is a changelessness about the Word and the message. But there is equally a demand to make that message relevant in a changing world. Missionaries are constantly having to battle with cultural differences and to decide what is part of the essence of the Gospel and what is merely the cultural accretion which we have accepted in the Western world.

The Keswick Convention in its second century has to be very careful in this particular area. There are many who would want the Convention to modernise itself in such a way that it becomes an exciting vanguard of Christian experiment. Others just want things to remain as they always have been without any change at all. Somewhere between lies the truth. In one sense its message must not change and in another sense the way in which it is conveyed, especially to the younger generation, needs to be seen to be relevant. It is possible to hear without hearing, to listen to a message that is eminently biblical but somehow does not relate to the world today. It is easy then to give assent without it changing us one little bit.

In the theme of mission and service we are committed to proclaim the call of God which in essence is the same today as it was for Isaiah or the early apostles. But we have to be honest and relate it to a vastly different world. It may well be that the style of the missionary meeting will change and the thrust of the challenge to service. Since this call to service is also linked with the great theme of holiness of life – and that is the burden of this book – there must also be that balance in the presentation of the call to holiness.

Holiness is inevitably a call to live a life set apart for Christ in the midst of the world. The old adage that we must be 'in the world but not of the world' is as clear as anything can be. That does not change. We will not adapt to the ideas and rapidly changing principles of our society. Even if we are thought to be old fashioned we hold on to biblical principles. But equally we are asked to wrestle with problems that the biblical writers could not know in their day and age. Some of the problems arise from the technological world in which we live, some from the rapid advances in science and medicine. How do Christians react and what is the outworking of Christian principles in these areas?

By and large the ministry of the Keswick Convention, like the ministry of every pulpit, is to proclaim the eternal principles and to encourage people to use their minds to work out what it means for them in their own situation. But the seminar movement has become very significant as Christians together seek to thrash out some of these issues. Practical holiness may well mean people with very different viewpoints talking through the application of those truths which we all share together. It is vital to keep the balance between the unchanging and the changing.

Using another metaphor, there is meant to be a rhythm in Christian living. I have never indulged in water sports of any kind and therefore hesitate to dare to relate the Christian life to the oarsman. But I am told on good authority that the boat only moves effortlessly forward when the oarsmen are in rhythm. I seem to recollect discussing with a friend who was in a university boat which sank what had gone wrong and he simply said that the rhythm had got lost. So instead of going forward they went downwards! That I believe to be true of Christian experience. If we lose the rhythm we are in danger of being blown about by every wind of new doctrine and every fresh idea which comes to us.

One of the rhythms in the Christian life is the coming in and going out. We have the rhythm of coming in to listen and going out to serve. In fact one should lead to the other. As we come into the presence of the Lord for worship and prayer we find the challenge to go out and share the good news. Once we are out in the world seeking to proclaim and to live out the Gospel, we are being driven to prayer and worship for the strength and renewal we need. That rhythm or balance is vital to healthy Christian growth both individually and as a church.

The inward movement of the rhythm is to be seen both in personal devotion and corporate worship. It means a constant openness to the message of God's Word and the ministry of God's Spirit. These must always go together. Word without Spirit can be hard and dead. Spirit without Word can be frothy and superficial and subjective. But in with the Word and the Spirit there will constantly be a call to go out in obedience.

Anglican readers will recollect that in the age-old tradition of the church we sang at Morning Prayer the Venite, Psalm 95. Change has inevitably come and this is no longer central in the worship of most churches. In some ways that is a loss. The Venite was a reminder of why we come to worship, with an opening section of praise and thanksgiving and a closing section on the dangers of disobedience and the possibility of wandering around in the wilderness. Sadly in some modern liturgies the Venite has been truncated and we only have the section on praise and worship. That is probably a reflection of our age. We are high on worship and low on obedience. The music which God delights to hear is primarily that which is seen in a life of obedient service, as in those challenging words of the prophet Amos: 'Let justice roll on like a river, righteousness like a never-failing stream' (Amos 5:24). Worship which is meaningful and pregnant with life will always include a call to obedience and a warning of the dangers of disobedience.

True worship will always be earthed in an awareness and confession of sin. Isaiah did not hear the call to service before he had the vision of the Lord which made him tremble and confess his utter unworthiness. God had to make his enthusiastic prophet see that he could only be fitted for service when he had learned the greatness and majesty of God and the complete insignificance of the prophet. He also had to learn that his lips were unclean and needed cleansing before they could be inspired. It is dangerously possible to challenge to service without preaching a message that will bring people low in penitence. God can only use a cleansed and sanctified vessel.

But there is no limit to what he can do through that kind of vessel. Nor should the message of sin and God's remedy for it ever stop short of a reminder that the ransomed sinner is not only right with God but right for service. Isaiah was eager and ready when he had been cleansed to offer himself for service. Peter after the incident on the lake when he had acknowledged his utter sinfulness was ready to become a fisher of men, and Moses was indeed rebuked because he complained that he was unfit for service, almost denying the efficacy of God's enabling for the task.

The outward movement in the rhythm will always bring us back. In the first place the task of a Christian is not just to be a gentle influence in society. We are called to make disciples and to baptise them in the name of Father, Son and Spirit. That is part of the final great commission of Jesus. We should never apologise that there is to be an in-drag in Christian ministry. We all recognise the danger of the Christian ghetto and we must fight against any attempt to keep Christians in some isolated community. But especially today with its challenge to Christian living there is a need to bring the convert into the fellowship of the church. That is why church growth matters and that is why some of us at least can rejoice that we are seeing people not only influenced for good, not only having a touch of the Christian spirit, but actually being

131

truly born again and added to the church of Christ. That is ultimately not the climax of missionary service but a great peak in it. Indeed in Christian service as we draw people into the family of God so our next prayer is that they too should go out and draw in so that the church may truly multiply.

But equally the balance of the out and in is seen in the Christian servant who needs constantly to come back for renewal and refreshment. Wherever Christians get engaged in mission there is an even greater need for a living fellowship to which they return. It highlights the tremendous importance of the home base of those who go out in overseas missions. Though not physically present with the community from which they come, they need the assurance of continuing prayer, contact and love. When we are thrown in at the deep end for Christ we are conscious of our need not only for his presence with us but for the encouragement of others. There is that famous exhortation in Hebrews 10:24-25 to remind us that we should spur one another on in love and good deeds and not give up meeting together. It is the experience of persecuted churches that there is great strength in unity and fellowship. We are not meant to go it alone.

When I was ordained my theological college gave me a Book of Common Prayer. Written within the flyleaf were the wise words of the Principal: 'The life of worship is the first essential for fruitful service.' I recollect that I had serious doubts as to whether I believed that statement and felt it was an attempt to keep us enthusiastic young ministers well within the Anglican fold and using the time-honoured liturgy. But the Principal had much more wisdom than I. My ministry has proved abundantly how right he was both for myself and for those to whom I minister in the church. In worship we should always be conscious of the world outside, both as we pray and as we ponder the truth of God's Word. In worship we are constantly being exhorted by the Word to go out and to work. In that way fruitful service will be the end product of the life of worship.

Going out is not only a synonym for missionary endeavour and evangelistic work. It is a reminder that we must work out the implications of our faith. Constantly the New Testament speaks in terms of the renewing of our mind. Far from warning that we can be too cerebral, the New Testament seems to insist that the greater danger is that we will become too unthinking. To read the letters of Paul is to recognise that he expected Christians in the early church to use their mind. When we wrestle with the great theology of Romans we need to be reminded that it was written as a letter to be understood and obeyed by those young Christians. He was not writing a treatise for preachers to come and for students of theology to write their doctoral theses. So clearly the mind is meant to be used and renewed. Peter uses the vivid phrase in 1 Peter 1:13 that we must 'roll up the sleeves of our mind'. He is using Eastern analogy about hitching up the robes when wanting to get on so that progress is not impeded. With untidy thinking we can never fulfil the demands of Christian living.

All of us, individually as well as corporately, must work out what it means to be a Christian in our day so that we may be consistent in ourselves and so that we may encourage others who find the going hard. Individuals have to work it out in their particular areas of service. The Christian doctor or the Christian businessman, the Christian MP, the Christian Trade Unionist – all of these and many more have to see what it means to be a Christian in their own sphere of life. So Paul reminds us that we have to work out our salvation because it is God who works in us (Philippians 2:12–13). We could not even begin to work it out without God's strength working in us. But God working in us wants to be quite sure that we work out that salvation and make it relevant, clothed with flesh and blood in the world of today.

Of special concern in our contemporary situation is the spiritual wellbeing of those called to leadership within the church in the ministry of the Word and in missionary service. There have always been tragic casualties and we are meant to expect this since the Bible is full of similar stories. But we must never be complacent and there is some evidence that for all kinds of reasons there is an escalation in the society of today. Ministers and missionaries and other full-time Christian workers, if that phrase may be allowed, need desperately to come back constantly for spiritual renewal. They need urgently the care and prayer of the people of God who are indebted to them for their ministry. Never before was this care more needed and never before did leaders need to be humble enough to accept help. I have always been impressed that the apostle Paul with all his dynamic leadership would ask often plaintively for the prayers and support of the people to whom he wrote. He would open his heart to them and was sad when they did not open theirs to him.

But there are ways in which those called to leadership may spiritually help themselves in finding time to be with the Lord, and time to get away from the normal routine of ministry and service to find strength in the Word of God and in the quietness of a relationship with him. There are great dangers in our age of self-pleasing and self-publicity. The devil is also very much roaring around seeking to bring down morally and spiritually those whom the Lord would use.

One of his most subtle weapons is to spread despair amongst those who would lead the church. We know from Scripture how a great man like Elijah could one moment be on the pinnacle of joy and then driven down into despair and even ready to take his own life. Many of us do not know quite that sudden shift of feeling, but all of us know it in part. What a liberation it is to recognise that we are not judged by other people, and even more importantly we do not judge ourselves, as 1 Corinthians 4:3–5 assures us. Every Christian minister should underline these words in his Bible and read them constantly. To know that the Lord knows us deeply and still loves us even more deeply is a motivation to go on in service when the devil would drive us to despair, sometimes for reasons that are very obvious and sometimes just out of sheer spiritual exhaustion. Every church should seek to enable their leaders to find this renewal. The ministry of a Convention like Keswick has no greater priority than to send back Christian missionaries and ministers renewed. Year by year these are the letters that cheer the heart of a Chairman of the Convention more than anything else. Some come weary and dispirited and go away renewed and reinvigorated.

Yet I suspect there is another malaise which needs the cure of the rhythm of New Testament Christian living. It is a subtly dangerous condition brought about by the expectation in our Western society that life should be easy and comfortable. We are constantly being reminded of our rights and Christians are not immune to this insidious teaching. It is possible to become self-pitying and Christians, not least those in leadership, can be found indulging in this dangerous practice. Sometimes it is the obvious result of over-work, disappointment and weariness. Elijah felt that he was the only one left but had to be shaken out of it by a caring but very challenging God. The answer to Elijah was not a word of easy comfort nor a suggestion of sabbatical rest but in fact a call to go back, to recog-nise that he was not the only one left and that there was a very urgent job to do.

There is nothing inherently wrong about Christians finding time for sabbaticals and special courses. It would be possible to read the lives of the saints of old and to be very critical of the spirit of our age. Some-how these men and women did not seem to care for this kind of reprieve from the insistent challenge of service. There is a value in times of study, refresh-ment and renewal of vision. Clearly training has its place and particularly so in a world where it is so com-plex to serve the Lord. But there is a temptation today to see this as almost essential to fruitful service. The Christian scene in the past and present demonstrates that very many people who never have all the full training, who never take advantage of sabbaticals and refresher courses are amongst the most effective ser-vants of the Lord. All of us need to be honest before God, to be true to our own convictions and above all to be faithful and sacrificial in service. The Lord who called us had nowhere to lay his head, did not think in terms of how much time he could have off, but gave himself utterly to his work and to people. The same spirit inspired men like the apostle Paul with his con-stant recitation of the badges of service not in terms of success but in terms of sacrifice and suffering. It easy to be pious at this point. It is just as easy to excuse ourselves living easily and comfortably. The grain of wheat that bears fruit must be ready to die.

Even the great theme of church growth can become an academic study, almost a growth industry in itself rather than that which follows from faithfulness to the Word of God and dedication in prayer. It is so difficult to assess statistically the growth of the Kingdom that statistics are almost valueless. How much missionary work of the highest calibre would be deemed a failure by any yardstick of statistics in terms of numbers of people converted. It would be not only untrue but desperately unkind to such men and women of God to suggest that they might have done loads better if they had understood all the secrets of church growth.

Once more the balance is important. We do need to recognise that there are lessons to be learned from growing churches. But the growth of which the New Testament speaks is primarily in terms of spirituality and likeness to Christ rather than numbers. When our Lord speaks in John 15 about the fruit which Christians will bear, he is clearly thinking more in terms of character than numerical increase. But it goes without saying that Christians are in the business of numerical increase since we long so much to see many people coming to faith and enjoying all the wonder of Christ now and the glory of heaven to come. But Jesus did remind us that few find the narrow road and therefore we need not become over-concerned about numbers at any time. Indeed they can become a great snare, as David discovered when his proud census led to stern words of judgement. The great balance of the prophet needs to be kept if we are to 'strengthen the stakes and lengthen the cords'. If we are about the business of deepening our knowledge of and love for the Lord and his Word, seeking to reach out lovingly with that

Word and for that Lord, we can leave the numbers to God. A church which grows numerically without growing spiritually is in danger and a church which has little concern for the outsider but is desperate for spirituality can become very arid and unattractive.

So the theme of this book has become clear. I believe it to be the pattern of Bible teaching and certainly that which inspires us at the Keswick Convention. There we have discovered over the years a pattern of teaching which God has seen fit to bless. There is nothing magical in the formula nor anything that is copyright to Keswick. After looking at the glory of God over the weekend we then appreciate afresh the awfulness of sin in the life of the believer and come to that place of repentance without which all else will be empty. Then we are reminded of the sufficiency of the sacrifice of Christ. The Cross is not just the beginning of Christian experience, it is the place to which we ever return both for judgement and for renewal. Then the Lordship of Christ is proclaimed. Not that we are called to make him Lord – he is Lord, whatever we do about him, Lord enthroned on high, bearing in heaven the marks of his suffering and with world dominion as his great goal. In the light of that Lordship we are then reminded of the fullness of the Spirit, not primarily for our satisfaction but for the fulfilment of the task to which the Lord has called us, in terms of both individual holiness and the extension of our Lord's kingdom.

Traditionally the Keswick Convention ends with that marvellous service of Holy Communion which often people see as the climax of all that we do together at the Convention. Indeed Communion at any time ought to be a marvellous climax and especially when we demonstrate unequivocally that we are all one in Christ Jesus. But even the beauty of a Communion Service, whether at Keswick or in our local church or in our home, needs to be seen in balance. Sometimes people have spoken about those lovely services being a foretaste of heaven and in a sense that ought to be true. One day in heaven we shall all gather in perfect fellowship around the risen Lord and here we do it in beautiful symbol. But it is more than that. It is very often a service in which we concentrate on the wonder of our Lord's atoning sacrifice and supremely the broken bread and outpoured wine speak of that event. We need to fight for the centrality of the once for all sacrifice of Jesus on the Cross remembered in communion. Some aspects of modern Communion Services have gone far away from that centrality. But in fact the Communion Service is even more than that. The Lord whose death we remember is now risen, ascended and glorified. Therefore our fellowship together and our recollection of the Lord's death which we proclaim in Communion until he comes should be an inspiration to go out in service in anticipation of the day of his return.

In many Anglican churches today the Communion Service will end with the exhortation: 'Go in peace to love and serve the Lord.' These words echo the language of Jesus. In fact a similar phrase comes in Luke 7:50 and Luke 8:48, spoken to two very different women. In the first instance Jesus spoke to a prostitute woman who had shown her love and faith in a quite demonstrative way. Jesus wanted to point out that her faith had saved her and that she was challenged to go into peace. Here it was a matter of a change of life and attitude which would be seen in days to come.

In the second instance it was a woman sick with a

haemorrhage of blood who had timidly touched Jesus, had been brought into the open and had been given these words of wonderful assurance that her faith had healed her and she was asked to go into peace.

In fact in the original the word for being saved in chapter 7 and being healed in chapter 8 is the same word. The needs were apparently different, yet deep down it was a symptom of the same problem. Both women were sent into a new relationship which would give them peace and make them agents of peace. Ultimately Christian mission and service are going into peace with the Lord and that concept comes very much from our Lord's words to the disciples before his ascension in John 20.

Peace is very much the theme of that dramatic Easter evening encounter in the upper room. Our Lord's first words to the gathered disciples were not just the formal Jewish greeting. They had a new meaning because of Calvary. He came to bring that peace which can only be found in the presence of Jesus. In order to bring it he had to break through shut doors. There was some excuse for those shut doors for those early disciples, still bewildered and uncertain. We have far fewer excuses for shutting our doors when we meet in Christian fellowship or cutting ourselves off in spiritual isolation. Never should the Christian family be cut off from the world, and even in worship we need to have the doors open metaphorically. Certainly the door of Christian fellowship should always be wide enough to admit all in need and open enough to be relevant to the world even as we pray. Through that shut door Jesus came to bring the kind of peace which exists in the midst of the world and its storms. We need to remember that Jesus could be asleep on the stormy lake and was somewhat distressed to discover that his disciples were fearful. When you are at peace within you can indeed smile at the storm. So Jesus burst through the shut doors.

Even more in that dramatic incident Jesus brought his peace into fearful hearts. Scripture clearly states that they were barred against the world 'for fear of the Jews'. It was a natural fear in the light of what had happened to Jesus. Somehow Jesus always seemed to be breaking down the fears of people and his 'fear not, it is I' was heard more than once. Never has the world been more fearful than today. Christians will inevitably share some of that fear and because of the toughness of Christian witness we may have our own brand of fear. These are not days for timidity. We have the promise of 2 Timothy 1:7 that God gives us not the spirit of fear but of courage and love and self-control. In order to find stability in the midst of natural apprehension we need to discover afresh the risen Jesus bringing his peace.

Looking at the passage in John 20:19–23, it is significant that Jesus repeated his greeting of peace. We can assume that this was more than accident. The second offer of peace was after he showed them his hands and his side still bearing the marks of his suffering. In a way this spelt triumph. Here was life through death. The passage says that they were overjoyed because they had seen the Lord and there was a great wealth of hope in that title given to Jesus. He was seen to be the victorious Lord. Death could not hold him. With that assurance for ourselves and for a world of need, we can have a new peace. Many people live with constant anxieties and fear because they have not discovered the answer to that problem of death which holds each one of us naturally in bondage. Through the risen Jesus and the Gospel he preaches we may have life through death. Already death has been conquered through death. These are words that the world needs to hear in order to find peace.

But the glimpse of the hands and side of Jesus were also a reminder that there was death in life. Even the risen Jesus bore the marks of his suffering and in the book of the Revelation when he is seen as victorious, he is also seen as the Lamb of God, slain from the foundation of the world. You may never escape the reality of the Cross. If we do not bow before the crucified Jesus now, we shall do it in judgement then. So there is no easy triumphalism in the Christian faith, but peace comes in the passion of Jesus. The price of life was his death and ultimately the price of sharing life is the willing self-sacrifice of the people of God.

Perhaps most important in that encounter in the upper room was the commission of the risen Jesus to send the disciples out into a world of turbulence with a new challenge to service and yet at the same time giving them peace in the doing of it. Following his reiterated greeting of peace Jesus says, 'As the Father has sent me, I am sending you.' It must have been a great reassurance to these disciples, especially to Peter with all his failure, to know that they were still useful and that the Lord still had a mission for them.

Indeed the experience of the risen Jesus has inevitably to lead to mission. The message had to be proclaimed and the proof of the risen Jesus to be seen in the new life of the disciples. So Pentecost would prove the complete change in the disciples when the Spirit enabled them to stand up and preach what they believed in theory. Even here in the upper room there is an anticipation of Pentecost as Jesus breathes on them and gives them a new authority in the power of the Spirit. So that balance remains. We are sent out with a message of peace and we are given strength for the task which humanly is beyond us.

Every year when ministering at the Keswick Convention, a preacher is conscious of a world of need outside the peace and beauty of this lakeside haven. Every preacher in the midst of a Christian fellowship, which should always be characterised by peace and love, will be conscious of a world of turmoil and strife, sadly often bursting into the very life of the church itself. There can be no greater commission than to go out with the peace of God and with the God of peace.

These two phrases come in Paul's closing chapter of his letter to the Philippians. In verse 7 he promises the peace of God which passes all understanding and in verse 9 he promises the God of peace. Before both of these phrases comes the little word 'and'. This reminds us that there is a condition of enjoying the peace of God and the God of peace. The first 'and' links back to the promise of what happens when we pray. Instead of being anxious, we are called to bring everything to God in prayer. The result will be the garrisoning of our hearts by the peace of God. The second 'and' links back to a challenge to obey the truth that we have learned and seen in action. We can only know the presence of the God of peace if we obey him and his Word. So it links back to that great commission which has been at the heart of this book when Jesus promised, 'I am with you always' – but only to those who go to make disciples.

It is a staggering thought that it is in obedience and faith that we actually discover the peace of God in our hearts and the God of peace in our lives. In that process the Christian who has found peace with God becomes an agent of peace and Jesus said 'Happy are the peacemakers, for they shall be called the children of God.'